Archway Publishing books may be ordered through booksellers or by contacting:

Archway Publishing
1663 Liberty Drive
Bloomington, IN 47403
www.archwaypublishing.com
1 (888) 242-5904

ISBN: 978-1-4808-2617-5 (sc)
ISBN: 978-1-4808-2618-2 (e)

Library of Congress Control Number: 2015921360

Print information available on the last page.

Archway Publishing rev. date: 3/9/2016

"Short Stories"
A book by John Caulfield

A Book of Short Stories put together by the Author.
His intention is to amuse the reader, provide a chuckle.
Hopefully he succeeds.

Dedicated to,
Jeanne, the love of my life.

For Dr. Katz

Slainte!

Dr. Jo Caulfield

N, joy

Table of Contents

Introduction

"Life in the fast lane"

Yesterday was full of thoughts of tomorrow.

Tomorrow is here.

"Life in the Fast Lane"

—⟋⟍⟍—

I'm 85. Retired. Life is good. Just a little slower. When it comes to cutting the grass it's a lot slower. When I was younger I cut the grass using an old temperamental self-propelled hand mower. On this big yard. Self-propelled, worked part time. Had to keep pulling the rope.

I have a riding mower now. All I have to do is turn the steering wheel. It does a good job with very little effort on my part. Of course I take full credit for a job well done.

Younger! When I was younger. A long time ago. I did a lot of planning, dreaming on how to fix the house, the property. Especially on weekends.

We bought a house in sad shape, needed a lot of TLC. It was what we could afford. We raised three kids in it and made the house a home.

Sunday evenings when I could do no more. I would sit right here on the hill under my apple tree. I'd relax with a beer and look down at the house and property.

I would dream of all I wanted to do. To fix. To change.

Didn't have much money so I had to do it all myself, by hand.

Years have come and gone. Some of the fixing never got done.

Now?? Now I am angry with age. Old age snuck up on me. One day I was old. My youth was gone. Never to return.

My mind is still young. I still dream. Things I'd love to do. My body? It won't respond. It's old. It's tired.

Awakening to the fact I can no longer fix and build things breaks my heart. Still I dream and plan. Maybe if I hit the lotto. Another dream.

Right now I still have half the yard to mow. I'll get around to it. Instead I'm watching a little white Butterfly flitter erratically in the air seemingly with do direction. It goes high low and sideways at the same time and yet it is going somewhere round about in the same direction.

I'm told it's not a Butterfly. It's really a Moth. I don't know. I like Butterfly. Watching this harmless creature I wonder why, what is its purpose? Does it know where it is going? Does it know where it is? Does it know where it's been?

Does it get tired? It seems to go in all directions at once yet seems to always move one way like it has a destination. When it gets to that destination does it know it has arrived?

Wait!!!!! From somewhere. Another identical Moth flying from where?

It flitters in all directions at once. Both Moths fly erratically in all directions. Miraculously they find each other. In midair they meet and kiss while performing the wildest maneuvers. They separate and flitter away amazingly in different directions. Erratically moving away from each other till their gone, sadly alone. Leaving me to wonder. What was that all about? How did they find each other?

What did they say to each other when they met? "Hang a left at the intersection to avoid construction. When you get to Aunt Cora's house tell her old Mister Caulfield is still dreaming under his apple tree."

Why are these harmless creatures here? Why was one going East the other going West before and after their kiss hello and goodbye? A Wonder?

I'm sure some College has a million dollar grant from the Government to study Moth behavior to discover its secrets. I don't want to know. Like the end of the world. Some things belong to God. Leave my Butterfly's alone, otherwise God will have no secrets at all.

I still have to finish cutting the grass, but, the Butterflies have left me with a mystery, requiring my full attention.

Maybe tomorrow. Life goes on.

Introduction

"Bon Voyage"

He floated down the river, frightened out of his wits to the amusement of all. A long time ago. The story is true.

Only a few people knew. I'm the last one. Now you.

Of course the embellishments are mine.

Set your sails, batten down the hatches. Jack sails again.

"Bon Voyage"

This is a story I don't know where to begin, 1943, 1944. It's a story about a bunch of boys, young teenagers coming from good hard working families.

We lived a few blocks from the East River, Queens New York City during World War 11. We didn't have many extras in life but we had plenty of what we needed, Family.

We didn't know what an allowance was. If we did know we would never ask because we knew our parents didn't have it to give.

There were six of us. We had low paying odd jobs after school where we made pocket money, pennies. There were six of us. If one guy had money we all had money. A friendship that lasted a life time.

In the summer when it got hot we would go to the city pool, if we could pay the admission. Other times when it got real hot we would swim in the river.

The East River is a fast moving band of water that separates Manhattan from Queens and Brooklyn. The River runs between the Long Island Sound / Atlantic Ocean and New York Harbor / Atlantic Ocean. Its currants are treacherous. There is an extra turbulent narrow strip in the River called, "The Hell Gate."

History has it many old sailing vessels met their demise in the Hell Gate.

Since the East River is connected at both ends to the Atlantic Ocean our astute, not too distant forbearers figured it was a great Sewer Pipe. So, a huge sewage system was created to dump New York City's raw sewage into the East River. The river would carry the sewage to the ocean. Every toilet was connect to the East River. I won't describe it.

The river moves in both directions depending on the tide. So the sewage moves back and forth finally settling to the bottom.

As a kid I use to hang out on the river edge by the big big sewer pipes. Throw stones at the river rats. Lots of fun. Most of the stones were gone, already thrown. The cops chased us. Hanging out by the river caused Infantile Paralysis's, they said. Before the cure.

There is a big rail bridge over the Hell Gate. The bridge is appropriately called, "The Hell Gate." There is another Bridge further down called the Tri Borough Bridge. The Tri Borough is for vehicle traffic.

On one side of the Hell Gate Bridge there was a cove in the river. We called it the "Hell Gate Cove." The cove was up stream of the sewer pipes. The cove was free of solid floating waste so it was said, "It's Clean." Free of solid waste, therefore, non-polluted. On hot hot days we use to swim in the cove.

Of course we knew. One day we were in the cove swimming, kibitzing when Jack showed up with a big inflatable tire tube. It was during World War 11. The tube was valuable. Where did he get it??? It was worn out, covered with patches. He wouldn't say where he got it. Got in the water with his tube and wouldn't let anyone use it.

We started to horse around, push the tube with him in it much to his displeasure. He couldn't swim, none of us could. We pushed too far. The tube got caught in the current. He wasn't too far out, at first. Laughing, we tried to get him back. Couldn't.

He started downstream, on his way pass Brooklyn to New York Harbor, to the Atlantic Ocean. Nautical miles away, screaming, arms waving. If he got caught in the fast moving middle currant he was gone. If the old tube leaked he'd go to the bottom singing Anchors Away.

We left the cove running street level along the river. Long distance. Trying to keep up. Under the Hell Gate along the Sea Wall at the Park. We were racing to a bigger cove much farther down where Liberty Ships anchored. He was going little faster than we could run. Just keeping up.

It was a beautiful day. Blue sky, sun shining. To an observer, seeing Jack streaming down the river, looked perfectly normal. No Cell Phones then.

Jack, sitting upright in the tube, gathering speed, happily yelling, waving to everyone. People on shore couldn't hear, his mouth moving, "Help, Help!!!" They waved back as he sailed by. All he needed was a captain's hat and binoculars. Under the Tri Borough Bridge..

As Jack approached the big cove he got caught in an eddy which brought him close to shore. We got there. He was going round and round in the slow moving eddy, out of reach, weakly paddling, yelling.

We waded out, dirty water, over our head, holding hands in the eddy, grabbed the tube, pulled him in.

Made more than one attempt. Jack going round and round. We had to wait each attempt for him to get close. Yelling to the frightened Jack that we were going to leave him if he didn't stop fooling around.

We were beat. Dead tired. All the running. Wading out to rescue him. Finally we got him to shore.

Standing there, looking down at him, still in the tube. We were proud. A swelling feeling of accomplishment. We risked it all. We saved him. He laid in the tube staring up at us, most hateful look.

Got up cursing us, horrible language.

The ungrateful bastard got up cursing, blamed us! Blamed us!! For his once in a life time excursion. Sailing down the river, under the two bridges! Blamed us. He had First Class accommodations on the tube, the only one on board! A Voyage to write home about! We had to watch and wave from shore.

It's been accurately said, you can't please everyone. Took his tube, dragging his tail, went home.

All agreed. Should have left the Som Bitch in the eddy, round and round.

Note;

Jack's voyage never made the Headlines. Just another neighborhood happening.

Introduction

"A Summer Day"

It happened a long time ago.

Today feels like yesterday.

Read the story, See if you agree?

"A Summer Day"

A City neighborhood. Apartment buildings. Five, ten stories high. No space between. No backyard. No front yard. Just a vestibule door to the sidewalk out front and the street. Families live in these buildings. Apartment dwellers. Small rooms. Share space. Thin walls between. Good people. Transient neighbors.

The year, 1946. Before TV, before Air Conditioning. Today's forecast? "Hottest day." No breeze. The sun beats down relentlessly. The building bricks are hot. Inside the heat is unbearable. All windows open, multiple fans running.

No relief, no escape.

Six teenage boys standing on the sidewalk in the shade of Quinn's corner candy store. "Gees, is it hot!!" "Over a hundred." "Look at the tar in the street. It's soft. Look at it!" Pointing. "The tars got bubbles in it! Bet you could fry an egg on the street." "I like mine scrambled." "Hey, I'll take a couple over easy with a side of fries." "I'll give you a side of shit." Willy giving them the finger going out to step on the bubbles.

Nick looking across the street at the empty sidewalk. "I can see heat waves." Mack raised his brows touching Nick's forehead. "You better lie down.

I read an article, if you see heat waves that's the first sign of Mirage-itis. Can be fatal." "Bullshit." "No foolen, Arabs in the hot desert get Mirage-itis just before they die from a double dose of clap." "Always with the wise cracks." "Only telling you what I read. Not even Penicillin can help." Johnny, shaking his head, "You didn't read the whole article. You have to get the clap from a camel. Camel clap. Common in Arabia. All the Arabs get it." Frank grinned, "Camel clap? Is that worse than Monkey clap? I hear a lot of Africans are dying from monkey clap." Willie, hands up shaking his head, "Monkey clap? Camel clap!?" "What's all this clap crap?" Nick, "Ask the clap expert." Jerking his thumb back to Mack.

Not a cloud in the sky. The Sun is overpowering. "God it's hot." Eddy pointing across the street at Murphy's Funeral Home. "The sun is shining in Murphy's window like a blow torch, Good thing he don't have any stiffs on display. They'd be well done." Looking at Frank with a grin, "How do you like your stiff, baked or roasted?" "Naw, He keeps the stiffs on ice in the freezer." "Ever see his freezer?" "No." "Then how do you know? Once their embalmed maybe they don't require refrigeration." "Who the hell cares?" "You ever wonder why they call it a Funeral Home? Hell of a home." "Murphy lives upstairs with his family. So it's his Home." "How the hell can you live in a house with a stiff down stairs, a strange stiff?" "Must be a bitch, get up in the middle of the night to take a pee. What do you do? Tip your hat." "You get used to it!"

No people walking on the sidewalks. Most people hiding indoors, windows open fans running full blast. A few people sitting out on their stoops in the shade under umbrellas. "Look at all the old ladies with their kitchen chairs sitting on the sidewalk in the shade of the big elm tree. Look at them, beating the air with fans. Too much work. Bet it don't help."

John, looking at the elm tree as if seeing it for the first time. "That tree has been there forever, before any of us was born. With admiration. Must be three feet in diameter." Shaking his head with a new sense of ownership.

"Beat up, scared old tree. Just stands there on the sidewalk next to the curb. Everybody abuses it. We all carved their initials in it, dogs pee on it. Can't kill it, shaking his head, not even the salt they put on the street in the winter can kill it. Raising his hands. Indestructible!" Johnny laughing, "Indestructible! Old Mister Asmonte tried to knock it down." They all laughed, "Old Mister Asmonte!." "He's gotta be at least 90." All talking at once. "Yeah, remember? Asmonte came home late from the Pizzeria." "Yeah, playing pinochle with his old Italian friends." "It was Columbus Day too! Remember? Celebrating with his Goombahs. Too much anisette with the Espresso's." "Backed his car into the tree. Up on the curb." They all laughed. "Poor old guy, sitting there in the car, door opened. Kept saying the tree moved when he backed up!" "His wife came out of the house like a banshee." "Yeah, grabbed him almost by the ear and dragged him in the house." "Kept bleating, the tree moved, the tree moved."

"I heard she's Sicilian. Tough, the worst kind." "No more anisette for him." "Talk about scars. He bumped that tree pretty good."

The neighborhood at a standstill, everything stopped. Hardly an automobile, no movement. It's an effort to just to breath. An empty City Bus turning onto Crescent Street shifting gears spewing out a stream of black exhaust. The Boys watch, the exhaust hung in the still hot air. "Can't be healthy." "Don't smell good."

Sunday afternoon. The boy's hadn't met early enough to catch the train to the beach. "God it's hot!" "Yeah, wiping his head. The whole month of July, a scorcher." "I read somewhere that one day the heat will melt the North Pole and New York will be submerged, under the ocean."

"Short walk to the beach." "Won't need a pool."

"Pool!!? Looking accusingly. We said we're going to the pool! What the hell are we standing here for? Looking at faces. Let's Go!" "It's a long walk." "Go by way of 20th street, shade most of the way." "Better than standing here! I'm going." Moving away. The others followed. The pool about a mile. Dragging themselves.

No rush in the heat.

In sight of the pool. They Stopped. "Holy mackerel!!! Look at that line waiting to get in the pool." Three abreast. "Never seen the line that long before." "Out of sight!" Looking at it didn't make the line any shorter. More people coming. They rushed to get on the end. Three abreast. The Women's line on the other side, just as long. They waited in the blazing sun. No shade, sweating, standing beside sweating strangers.

The line grew, more people came. Seemed like the new people in the back were pushing, closing the space between of them. They were crammed in a narrow space. Three abreast, between a rail fence and the side wall of the pool building. Long line, slow moving. Crunched, the people in the back keep pushing. Standing close to other people, strangers in the sweltering heat. Try not to touch other people's sweaty skin but still you did. There was no air, the line was suffocating, moving very slow. Running out of conversation, standing in silence, listening to other People. Suffering, with thoughts of nothing, heat dumbing the senses, slowly moving forward. Finally, finally they moved up just before the Pay Window five feet away. Park attendant maintained the distance. They had their admission ready in their sweaty palms.

A Park Official came out his office and closed the big gate in front of them.

"That's all folks, we're full up, no more room." "What!? no way!" The boys shouted, pushing their arms through the gate. The attendant held his hands palms up, grimaced. "No more ankle Tags, gotta close it's the law." He left the boys standing with their arms stretched out. Going back to his fan cooled office. The boys were stunned, looking at the retreating Attendant. The long wait. The heat of the day putting their minds in a stupor. "CLOSED."

They were shocked awake, helpless. The people in back of the line still didn't know. The word was passed back. There was a loud groan. Some nasty language as the people squeeze out of line between the fence rails.

The Boys were furious. They were there, at the Pay Window, almost in the pool.

They had their admission in their hand. Ready to hand it over. "CLOSED." The boys looked at each other. On hot days if you didn't catch the train to the beach there was nowhere else but the pool.

"Closed." This had never happened before. The full impact hit them. "Closed." no Pool! Their frustration grew in all directions.

Anger, looking through the closed fence. No place to go! Individually their minds focused on the park attendant. That rat, he seemed to enjoy closing the gate right in front of them. He had a spiteful smirking smile on his face looking at them as he snapped the lock. They looked in his office window. He was nowhere to be seen. They gave the window the bird.

For a few helpless moments, the thought of storming the Gate, climbing over and rushing inside. The thought passed with reluctance. Helpless. The boys, not altogether, resigned themselves. No pool today! Shit, Shit, Shit!

"Whose idea was that!? In a loud challenging voice. Whose idea was that!?" "Go to the pool, instead of the beach!? Whose idea was that!?" No one answered.

No Pool. Seems like the day just got hotter. They were there. Standing in front of the closed pool entrance. No place to go.

The other line people, dispersed walking away dejectedly. No place to go. The Guys just kinda moved away aimlessly trudging up steps to the Pool's outside Observation Deck.

On the Deck, glaring sun, no other people, too hot. They were all alone in the heat. Looking down into the pool was a torture. They could see all the lucky people in the pool splashing in the water. Water, that was the only difference between them. Water. It made one group happy and the other miserable.

The miserable group was them, on the outside, looking down. They stood there motionless, in the heat, looking at the people in the pool. Frankie, with resignation, talking into space, "This is really dumb. We're standing here in the blazing sun looking at people enjoying themselves in cool water. Let's get the hell outta here." Still they stood. Leaning forward resting their arms on the hot metal fence rail with one foot up on the lower rail, motionless, speechless. They looked. The pool they are looking at is a big, big Olympic size pool. A pool about a city block long, a half a city block wide. The pool is 6 feet deep at one end tapering to about a foot at the other end so kids of all sizes can swim. At one end, separate from the Swimming Pool is a Diving Pool. Sixteen feet deep. Overhanging the Diving Pool is a huge 33 foot high tower with a diving platform at the top. Two 26 foot platforms sticking out each side with one 16 foot platform below in the middle with steps going to the top. The other end of the long swimming the pool is Kiddies Wading Pool. All around the whole pool are three foot wide concrete sunning decks foot and a half high. The decks laid out like wide steps, stepping up eight decks high.

On this hot day the Pool is full. Full of happy people. Many bathers lounging on the sunning decks. The deprived boys looked. Revenge in their hearts.

"Look at that bastard, thinks he's Superman." Nick pointing at a portly, partially bald, middle aged guy who was innocently stretching his arms. "Looks like he's posing for a Muscle Magazine. Som bitch." The outside anger was growing.

Mack observed, "There's got to be at least a two thousand people in the there." No matter where they looked people were having fun. Splashing each other, laughing, hollering. Completely wrapped up in themselves ignoring the suffering of the Guys outside looking down.

The boy's resentment grew. Looking down at all the selfish people having fun. The haves and have not's. Nick said, "The bastards," pointing down, "There has got to be some way to get even with them." "Yeah, Mack imagined storming medieval castles, we could pour hot oil down on them." This thought or one similar passed through more than one head.

The boys looked at the whole pool.

The pool is self-enclosed. Surrounding the outside of the Pool is a sixteen foot high brick wall. The wall surrounds the pool like the Great Wall of China. On top of the wall is an 8 foot high steel bar fence. The wall and fence are supposed to keep people out. They do.

"Let's go." No place to go. The boys moved away. Aimlessly walking to the other end of the Deck. The other end is the beginning of the sixteen-foot high brick wall that surrounds the pool.

They all saw it, paused. A moment's reflection. Without a word, all together, they walked to the wall where it joined the Deck. No one spoke.

They had all climbed out onto that wall many times when they were kids. It looked different now, smaller but still dangerous.

When they were Kids, they would climb out off the Observation Deck where they were now standing. Swing on the Deck railing, flipping themselves up onto the top of the wall. Grab the rail fence before falling backwards sixteen feet below. They were kids, they had no fear. Frank said, shaking his head looking at the wall, "I wouldn't climb out there now. How the hell did we do it, we must have been crazy." "We were." They all reflected.

"Hey, remember Tarzan?"

Tarzan! The thought got an instant response from everyone. "Tarzan! Wow, he was something." The heat of the day forgotten.

Tarzan! With almost comic book superman reverence. They all visualized a man from their childhood. A man they called Tarzan. Tarzan! Inside their minds they were all looking at the same fantastic memory. It was all crowded together. A memory of one unforgettable summer when they were kids.

Tarzan! All board smiles. "Remember Tarzan?" At the mention of Tarzan, each had his own memory of the same event, different but yet the same.

They were kids, little kids, runts, and Tarzan was their superman. As runts they would climb up on the brick wall outside the pool and move along the wall holding on to the rail fence to the diving pool side. They would stand there wearing nothing but their faded bathing suits and look in. Look at all the people in the Pool swimming, having fun.

They were outside looking in because they didn't have the price of Admission, 11 cents. The year was 1941. The Great Depression. Times were tough. They all had bathing suits on because occasionally a fireman would come into their neighborhood and turn a fire hydrant on in the street outside the Park for them to play.

Play in the water spouting out of the fire hydrant. When the pressure was high the water would push you half way across the street tumbling and falling down on the hard asphalt. Had to be careful of the traffic. The Cars would drive right through the water and the kids. Weren't that many cars in 1941.

A fire hydrant turned on, spouting water and nothing else. Didn't take much for kids to have fun.

The kids never knew if the hydrant would be on or off but they all came in their well-worn swim suits just in case. Some of us wore ragged short pants.

If the hydrant wasn't open the Kids would hang around and wait. Wait for the Fireman to come and turn it on. More times than not the Fireman didn't come. Some of the kids would go into the Park. Climb the pool wall and stand or sit with their legs between the bars without lunch for hours looking in at the pool waiting, waiting for the fire hydrant. The only blessing they had was the trees planted outside along the wall provided shade.

Just about every day when the fire hydrant was closed there would be a line of Kids standing on the wall, or crouched down looking in at the pool. Occasionally the Parkies would stand down on the ground and try to chase the kids off the wall. "Come on Kid, get off the wall." The Kids would stand closer to the fence and just look down at the Parkies. The Parkies couldn't reach them. The Kids knew they were safe, they didn't move. The Parkies made threats, sometimes pretty strong threats. The kids knew they were safe so they just looked down. Occasionally a Parkie would go inside the Pool to chase the Kids. The Kids would move to safety but would come back. Guess this made the Parkies mad. The Parkies would make more threats, give up and leave. The life guards inside the pool were busy watching the people swimming, never bothered.

Then came Tarzan. Tarzan, each boy remembered was a tall blonde-headed, good looking guy. A natural Adonis. Like a Greek god. He had a tremendous build with a terrific smile. Beautiful to look at but distant. Don't know how tall he was but to a little kid looking up he was a giant.

Some thing all kids knew about him, unspoken, a feeling, that he was someone to be feared. No one really knew what Tarzan did for a living. He spoke with authority when he spoke. He was always well dressed and seen with nice looking women. He would come into the park alone to meet with other men but nobody ever asked. It was rumored by older people that Tarzan was a mob enforcer, a real tough guy. Those things didn't mean anything to kids. To the kids Tarzan was a God and the kids all liked him. Why? Why did the kids like Tarzan? Simple, because Tarzan liked kids. When he had the time he'd toss a ball around with you or show you the right way to stand in the batter's box, and how to hit. He was well dressed and smelled good and always smiled at you, say Hi. Sometimes making a feinting motion like a boxer ready to hit you. When Tarzan did like that it made a kid feel like a giant.

Hard to explain why kids like anyone. But all the kids liked Tarzan.

Kids respected him too. The kids knew never to get too familiar and it was understood no one ever called him Tarzan to his face. No one ever asked how he got the name Tarzan, he was just Tarzan.

One hot summer day Tarzan was in the Park. It was a hot day like so many other hot days in the city. What made this day different to Tarzan is anybody's guess. Tarzan was seen standing alone with his jacket off in the shade of a tree waiting for someone. People never approach him. I guess he saw all us kids lined up on the wall staring in at the pool. No one knows how it happened but all of a sudden Tarzan was on top of the wall. He walked out holding on to the bars to where the kids were. "We all moved away looking at him amazed he was up there with us."

"Yeah! Remember? We didn't know what to expect! Was he going to throw us off the wall?" Frankie looking at the rest of the guys, "Remember how scared we were?"

The moment recalled, livid, each to his own memory. They remembered Tarzan standing like a giant. In front of them. He let out a yell, a lions roar. He used his tremendous strength to bend the bars in the fence. He bent them wide enough so we kids could slip between. He bent the bars right in front of the Life Guards inside the pool and Park Attendants outside the pool, and everyone else. He bent the bars with a defiant grimace changing to a smile plainly enjoying himself. The Life Guards and Parkies turned away so they didn't see.

Tarzan stood there while all us kids slipped between the bent bars and ran away into the pool. No one stopped us. Had to be a runt to squeeze between the bars. No one was fat in 1941.

I remember grinning up at Tarzan as I squeezed between the bars and him giving me a wink. After all the Kids had snuck in, Tarzan left. The Parkies and lifeguards got their nerve back and started catching kids, late comers, trying to squeeze in after Tarzan was gone. They were pretty rough on the kids that they caught. The Parkies said if they catch us we were going to jail.

"I told my Father" He laughed and said he wasn't going to bail me out. "They could keep me."

Going to jail? That didn't stop us, we kept trying. That was the beginning of a summer of sneaking in. If you didn't have eleven cents you could to sneak in. We didn't have eleven cents. The fire hydrant was still opened sometimes but we weren't there. We were on the wall, ready.

That summer, sneaking in the pool became a challenge.

Not all Kids were willing to try. Afraid of climbing out on the wall or afraid of getting caught. Only the kids with the nerve to try would be standing on the wall and we would stand tall. A select group. The other kids looked up to us. There was comradely between the kids who stood on the wall. A little boisterous as only kids can be to impress littler kids.

After a while we kids developed a sneak in system. Each day the Kids would line up single file on the wall by the bent bars. Sometimes a Parkie would be inside the pool by the bent bar. He would chase the kids off the wall. Kids, had all day. We would wait for the Parkie to leave and climb back. Frankie, laughing shaking his head, "We must have been a royal pain in the ass. Those poor Parkies, getting paid to take care of the park spending their time chasing kids."

Nick added quietly, "We weren't bad kids." All agreed.

The Life Guards were told to stop us sneaking in. They started chasing us.

The Challenge? There was a trick to it. A line of kids, maybe seven or eight, in their swim suits all standing on the wall against the fence looking in at the pool. The fastest runner would stand first in line at the bent bar. At the right moment when the life guards weren't looking he would slip between the bars and run. He would run as fast as he could on the concrete steps, between the people sunning themselves. Jumping over people, baskets and towels, heart pounding with a Lifeguard chasing him. He would run as far and as fast as he could. Little legs pumping. Down the steps to the water, dive head first into the six foot high water and stay under as long as he could. Lungs bursting. Under water, paddling as long as he could, hoping the Guard chasing him would not follow. They never did. While the first kid was running, leading the lifeguard away, many of the other kids would slip between the bars and disappear into the pool. The other lifeguards wouldn't follow them. They would look menacingly at the kids but their attention was focused on the people swimming. The kids would keep doing this till they all were in the pool.

Once in the Pool, the Kids never got out of the water. The lifeguards and Parkies would walk around looking for the kids without the elastic ankle tag. The kids would spend the entire day in the water. Wrinkle up like a prunes soaking in the water for hours. We loved it. Of course there was always the problem of peeing. The kids couldn't get out of the water to go to the Men's room, they might be caught without an Ankle tag. So if you saw one of your friends standing still in the water with a serious expression on his face. You knew he was peeing and you got away from him quick. The other people in the water around him didn't know the pee sign so they stayed and enjoyed the water. No problem, Chlorine took care of it. Kills everything, so they said.

Nick said with a degree of reverence, "Hey John, remember the time the Life Guards ganged up on you?" Hesitantly, "Yeah, I remember." Nick shaking his head. "That was scary."

John eyes closed. It came back. A kid again, standing on the wall. Surprising how clear the memory was. "Yeah I remember. We were on the wall. It was my turn. You bastards, looking at them, kept pushing me to slip between the bars."

"I wasn't ready. I remember. One Life Guard, was watching me out of the corner of his eye. The same one I had gotten away from the day before. He was fast, almost caught me."

"Hurry up!" I hear you Guys yelling, "Hurry up, hurry up!" "Aw right, Aw right! That Life Guard's watchen. He's watchen."

"Hurry up, hurry up!" "I didn't want to go. You guys were pushing. I squeezed between the bars. I remember the Life Guard coming. He had been watching, coming fast."

"Run, Run!" I hear you guys yelling, the last thing I remember. "Run, Run!" Eyes closed. "Like it was yesterday. I can feel the Life Guard right behind me. Gaining on me." "Run! Run!" Face contorted, chin tucked in, arms pumping. Running between people, past people, over people, over baskets, towels. Terrified, 'Run! Run! Don't trip! Don't trip! Run, run, run! Dashing down the steps heading to the water. People everywhere. The Guard is gaining. Closer, I can feel him reaching for me. Holy Mackerel!!!! There's a Big Life Guard at the water's edge waiting. They ganged up on me!' Life Guard running behind, reaching out. People all around. Running for the water. Big Life Guard waiting. The Guard behind yelling, almost has me. I see the Guard in front crouch down moving back and forth legs spread arms outstretched waiting for me. Running straight at him. I see his face, sun glasses, grinning. What do I do??? Instantly, dodged right. Dive left. He's reaching for me! I'm in the air between his legs so low my legs and feet drag on the wet tiles. I can feel his hands sliding on my back. I'm in the water!!! Under the water!!! Lungs Bursting. Peddling as fast as I can. Pain in my chest. Need air. Surface to get a mouthful of air, under again. Heart is pounding. Chest hurts. Surface for more gulps. Overhead water, on tip toes. Bouncing. Gasping for air. Bouncing up and down to lower water.'

Alone with his memory. Momentarily lost in the past. It came back so vividly John actually feels his heart racing. "I'll never forget it."

Looking at his friends accusingly. "All you bastards snuck in while two Guards were chasing me."

Shaking his head pointing at Nick. "Talking about close calls. Remember the time the Parkie caught you? You both went into the water." Nick smiling. "I had to poop. Couldn't do that in the water. The Parkie caught me coming out the men's room. I kept pulling, jumping. He fell in the water, shoes and all.

John said, "Poor guy, just trying to earn a living, chasing kids."

"Yeah, well he scared the crap out of me." Smiling, "Good thing I didn't have any more poop left."

"I saw him couple years ago on Steinway Street. He didn't recognize me." "Hell, I hardly recognize your ugly face from yesterday. Do you realize how much we've changed since we were those little runts?"

Frank shaking his head, "God, we were small! Sneaking in the pool with the big Life Guards and Parkies ready to pounce, we had guts."

Kids 10, 11 years old standing on the wall outside the pool looking in. Safe one minute with your friends on the wall. Once you slipped between the bars you weren't safe anymore. On your own. No one could help you. With your heart pounding, running away. Life guard after you. Running through the crowd of people any one could have grabbed you. Breathing hard, frightened out of your mind, any second they'll grab you. Diving into the water, over your head, holding your breath against your pounding heart, trying to stay under water as long as possible. Come up gasping for air on tip toes bouncing up and down gulping air moving toward shallow water.

But you made it! You were in the pool. You still had to stay under water and hide behind people till it was safe. Then wait for the rest of your friends to sneak in. Watch your friends sneaking in one or two at a time running away from a pursuer in different directions across the concrete sunning decks, down onto the wet slippery tiles crowded with people picking out a place to dive between the people and then dive head first into water over your head.

Sometimes your friends got caught but not all of them. The ones who got caught would be taken to the Office and questioned. The Parkies would get a Cop to scare you and threaten to call your Mother. Hell, no one had a phone at home in those days. In a few days the kid would try again.

Sneak in, you and your friends were pool brothers for the day. Swimming between each other legs underwater with your eyes open, doing flips and piggy back fights. Swallowing mouthfuls of chlorine water.

To sneak in the pool was a fright. To spend the whole day playing and peeing without food was heaven, we loved it. At the end of the day when the pool closed we kids would walk out through the main entrance broad shouldered. Shoeless, wearing just bathing suits with our eyes burning from the chlorine, happy grins on our faces, all peed out. We'd get our sneakers where they hid them in the park and go home. A stream of young squirts leaving the pool worn out after a day of illegal swimming with ravenous appetites ready for tomorrow. Mack said, sadly. "Sneaking in. It only lasted one season." "Yeah! whaddaya expect? Next year we're too big we weren't runts anymore."

"Hey wait a minute! Frankie with wonder, no kids ever tried to sneak in the next summer! No kids ever tried to sneak in again!"

"Yeah that's right. That means the new kids could pay their way, they didn't have to sneak in." "Yeah, the War was on. People were working, they had money." Frankie enthused, "Well I guess that makes us the Champs. Gotta be." Looking at the other guys puffing out his chest. He shouted to the world. "Ladies and gentlemen I wish to make this announcement." Spreading his arms to include his friends. Throwing back his head, "We are the champs!!! When we were Kids. Ten eleven years old. We challenged the mighty Pool Establishment and won!! We! Extending his arms again, smiling, we snuck in the Pool and they couldn't stop us."

Frank looked at the Guys. "Think of it! The pool being closed today. No big deal! If we were eleven years old we would sneak in. They couldn't stop us. Think of it! They wouldn't let us in today. Yesterday we got even with them for today." All smiling. A sense of satisfaction. Sneaking in. They never thought of it before. There never was reason to think of it.

Now, there was a sense of pride. More than just sneaking in made them proud.

It's that they were just little kids at the time. They developed a sneak in system. A little kid system. They persevered, they couldn't be stopped.

Now they were off the Deck on the ground looking up at the wall, the fence. Amazingly, the bars, where still bent! The memories flooding back.

The bent bars, a testament to them. To their achievement.

Only they could appreciate it. No one who hadn't been there, who hadn't tried to sneak in could appreciate it. Little kids had worked together to beat a system, and they won!

Mack held up his fist in a strong voice. "It's an epoch. It's a story to be told and retold forever."

The heat of the day forgotten. They laughed, shaking hands with feign puffed out chest, Admiration. It felt good.

"Hey! How come none of the life guards never jumped in the water after us? Did you ever think of that? None of them ever did.

"It was the sun tan lotion, Mack said. They didn't want to wash off the sun tan lotion or mess their hair.

Those guys, the life guards, were like bronze statues strutting around in front of the girls all day. They didn't want to get wet."

"You know, you're right. I never thought of it." "Maybe I'll try to get a job as a life guard and get me some girls." "First you gotta learn how to swim." "I can swim." "Like a lead balloon." "Ya gotta save people too. Ugly people who drown. Give them mouth to mouth." "I don't like that mouth to mouth." "Yeah, neither do I. Maybe I'll pass."

The small talk ended, they were standing on the Terrace steps looking at the wall thinking about yesterday with creeping melancholy. Unspoken, there was a moment of silence. Each one looking at his own thought's, memories. Climbing the wall, the frightening episodes of sneaking in. Slipping between the bars, a scared kid running with all of his might. Hearts pounding, almost getting caught. The good old days when they were runts, Tarzan bent the bars and they snuck in. It was a game they played when they were little. They won most of the time. A special memory. Seemed like a long time ago. Most of them still got a quiver thinking, almost getting caught.

"Hey! How did Tarzan get up on the wall to bend the bars?"

"He flew!"

"Yeah, maybe he did."

EPILOGUE

Twice the Parkies wired a piece of cyclone fence over the bent bars.

The older teen agers would remove it late at night and wire it to the Parkies Field House door.

The same teen agers who a few months later would be in the Service of their Country fighting WW11.

The life guards gave up and made only token chases. We were young kids with freedom to miss behave. What a beautiful country.

An enduring memory. I am the last one. I'm giving the story to you.

PS, We did take days off.

Astoria Pool, Look it up.

Introduction

"Martha"

Good kitchen help is always hard to find.

"Martha"

Mary sitting at Jesus feet listening to him teach his many followers. Martha calls out from the Kitchen, "Hey Mary, I need some help in here!"

Jesus admonishes Martha, "Let Mary be. She is doing the right thing."

At that Martha comes storming out of the Kitchen. Apron around her waist, sleeves rolled up, hair messed, sweat on her brow.

She spots Jesus preaching to everyone from the other side of the room. Makes a bee line across the room, past tables and chairs crowded with enraptured listeners.

Stopping in front of a seated Jesus. Looks down at him, takes a half-eaten Ham and Swiss out of his hand. Throws it in the garbage announcing to everyone in the room.

"Listen-Up!!!, Everybody! This is a BUFFET! Self-serve! No table service!" Pointing to Mary, "The Waitress is laying down on the job."

In a strong threatening voice shaking her fist at everyone. "Don't make a mess, no dumping on the floor. This is a respectable joint."

"Another thing! The next time you Guys come here to hear this Guy talk jerking her thumb over her shoulder back to Jesus, bring your own lunch. The Room Rates are on the Door if you're staying the night. We don't have a liquor license so do your wine drinking and carousing outside. No women upstairs after eleven. Clean your own chamber pots and don't forget to turn out the lights!"

"If you need anything, I'll be at Murphy's Bar and Grill across the street. I got a Union Job at Murphy's playing the Sax during Happy Hour 5 to 6." Walking to the door, checking an empty Tip Can, with a salute. "Ciao!"

The door slams. Jesus asks his apostles, "Murphy's? Is that a nice place?"

Peter, "I like the Sex." "She said SAX !!"

A yawning Mary wakes up, "Did I miss anything?"

Introduction

"Newspaper Boy"

I wrote this story.
I have no idea where came from.

"Newspaper Boy"

—∞—

In London on a bitter cold snowy night. The wind blowing icy stinging blasts. A young boy fumbles with the knob on a door to a Public House, a Pub.

The rags wrapped around his hands do little to keep the cold out and cause his hands to slip on the icy knob.

Under one arm he carries a roll of newspapers making it difficult to turn the knob.

The missing buttons on his tattered coat allow it to fly open to the cold wind when his hands are occupied.

Inside the Pub a line of middle aged and older gentlemen convene, standing and sitting at the bar. Warm and secure, each talking to his neighbor in low tones unconcerned with the world about them.

Resting comfortably on a stool at the furthest end where the bar turns to meet the wall is the most Senior gentleman of the group. He, due to senior status has this place of honor where he can survey all. This gentleman's attention is suddenly called to the door when it opens.

The little Newspaper Boy hurries in with a blast of cold air and a gust of snow. The boy quickly closes the door. The bar patrons are only momentarily distracted. Without a word they briefly examine the Boy. Dismiss him, turning back to their conversations to completely ignore him. The old gentleman watches as the little newspaper boy hunches his shoulders to shiver off the cold. Flap his loose coat tails to shake off the snow.

The old gentleman sees the boy is poorly clothed in rags. The rags are surly without warmth.

His shoes wrapped in rags are clearly worn out. His face is red from exposure, lips turning blue. The old gentleman knows that the Pub Manager will put the boy back out into the night and the cold.

The old gentleman watches as the boy approaches each patron at the bar one at a time. Tug lightly on each sleeve and looking up into disinterested eyes asks in a weak pleading whisper, "Buy a paper sir?" Without a word each patron shakes his head "NO" and turns away. The old gentleman observes all this and watches the boys desperation grow. Finally the boy reaches the old gentleman, tugs on his sleeve. Looking up into his eyes asks, "Buy a paper sir?" The old gentleman looking down at the boy asks, "What's the matter little boy, No Papa?" The little boy looks up and with water filling his eyes shakes his head, No. The old gentleman asks, "No Mama?"

The little boy blinks his eyes. Tears run down his cheeks. Shakes his head, No.

The old gentleman pats the little boy on the shoulder.

"Poor bastard."

EPILOGUE

You have to appreciate dry humor to enjoy that story, most people don't.

If the story depresses you look at the bright side.

The young Newspaper Boy grew to become a very sharp business man. He cornered the newspaper business and other industry and became independently wealthy.

For his own entertainment he purchased that same Pub.

He put up a full size colored photo of his nude rectum on the wall, waist high. Any patron who stoops down and kisses the photo gets a free beer.

The demand almost exceeds supply and the photo must be wiped daily. A better ending?

Introduction

"New York Satire"

On the Dark Side

I wrote this story to poke fun at Psychiatrists.
Easy to do. Also the people who live
life every day. There are so many.

"New York Satire"

On the Dark Side

Down Town Manhattan. A pleasant spring afternoon. Cloudless sky, warm sun, birds in flight, nesting.

On the street below. Turmoil! Fire Engines, Police, Ambulances, Bull Horns. Like a rollicking New Year's Eve on Times Square. Crowds of people, all looking up, waiting for the ball to drop.

It's not New Year's Eve. Not 42nd Street. No joyful cheering, No celebration. Still, there is a quite excitement in the air, it can be felt.

A lone figure of a man stands on a building ledge 5 stories up. Arms resting on the building facade. A Jumper.

"Ooops! Excuse me." A young man exiting the Subway in a hurry bumps his attaché case into my thigh dropping a small paper bag. Looking excitably, side to side.

"Has he jumped?"

Seeing the onlookers crowded around, all looking up.

Shaking his head, deep sigh, "Noooo, he hasn't jumped!"

Spreading his arms, with sarcasm. "The ghouls are all here, waiting."

Looking at me. Waving his arm. "How the hell am I going to get over there?

Pointing to the jumper. Get through this crowd of gawking Hyenas."

I Shrugged. His distain directed towards me, arms out, encompassing all. "I have to get over there!" With this remark I gave him a closer look. Young man, mid-thirties. Dressed in a smart tan, not off the rack Business suit. Dark brown hair, nice features. In good physical shape, an exerciser, about six foot. For some reason he wanted to get over to the jumper. His remark was full of contempt for the viewer's blocking his way. And I think to excuse his own lack of resolve because he made no attempt to push his way through.

He was talking to me. I felt obliged to reply.

"I don't think the Police will let you get much closer. I'm sure they have the area roped off. They don't want anyone injured when the Guy jumps.

"He won't jump!" Said with conviction. I looked at him again, with a little sarcasm of my own.

"You know that for a fact? You know how this movie ends?"

He looked at me with impatience. Making no effort to conceal his contempt explained.

"The World Renowned Psychiatrist, Doctor Olga Leapoffski has devoted her whole life to the study of Jumping Suicide." "She has written several books on the subject."

"No kidding?"

"That's right! She states that if the Subject does not jump within the first 15 minutes, they will not jump. A Jumper will wait and allow themselves to be talked "Down" or "In" as the case may be."

"Leapoffski? Sounds Russian." Defensively, "She is, lives in Moscow."

I said with an inquiring voice, "They don't have many tall buildings in Moscow. I don't remember hearing of anyone jumping off the Kremlin." Casting a stern look with raised brows. "Nevertheless, she has studied the Subject worldwide. She "Is," the Foremost Authority. And people do not jump off the Kremlin!"

Looking up I said, "I see people up there talking to him from a window."

"Amateurs."

"Hey! You know so much. Maybe you should be over there with the Jumper telling him about Olga."

"That's where I am supposed to be. 'I', said with pomp, 'I' am a Psychiatrist. I am a member of the City's 911 Emergency Psych Unit. It is our task to take charge in situations like this. Direct the Emergency Response Units. Reason with the Subject. Use our skills to change the minds of would be Jumpers." In a whisper I barely heard, 'What minds they have.'

"And that is why, I! must get through this Mass of miserable humanity."

"Well you're sure getting a late start. What happened? You didn't get notified in time?"

"Nooooo, said with raised eyes brows, I was notified in time. I was on my way out for lunch when the call came in, it was about 11:30 this morning."

"11:30!? This morning!!!???" With an impatient sigh. Slowly shaking his head. "We just don't accept calls without verification. All calls must be checked out before we, "I" take action."

Looking at my watch, it was now three thirty. He saw my questioning expression.

"As I said, if they don't go in the first 15 minutes they won't jump. The call about the Jumper came at a very inopportune time for me." My questioning expression did not change.

"You see I hadn't eaten breakfast, I was famished. It was Lunchtime and these things, 'Talk Downs' take time.

If I responded at once who knows when I would get a chance to do lunch." "Couldn't you grab a candy bar outa a machine?"

"No that wouldn't work. I once tried to eat my lunch, a Hero Sandwich, while talking to a Jumper. The only way he would come in off the ledge was for half my Sandwich."

A faraway look, "And what a sandwich it was. A terrific Hero on great Italian bread. With real Italian salami, capicola and provolone. Just the right amount vinegar and oil, extra virgin, grated cheese, mild peppers. The kind of sandwich you hate to finish."

From his description I was starting to salivate, I've known Hero's like that. "Well I gave him half the sandwich and when he came in off the ledge he wouldn't pay for it. Ungrateful Bastard!

The EMS left his hands free so he could finish the Hero in the Ambulance on the way to the Hospital.

He waved the unfinished sandwich at me through the window with the oil and vinegar running down his arm. Looney Toon smile on his face as they drove away. I'll never trust another Jumper. Had to add extra to my expense account."

"I bet you tried to overcharge him."

"Well, there was a delivery fee, I brought the sandwich to him."

He saw my disbelief and changed the subject back to being late.

He continued, "Anyway, as I said I was on my way out to do lunch when the call came in.

My building is directly across the street from the Jumper. I could see him plainly on the ledge."

"Unbelievable! You saw him on the ledge!?"

"That's right. My examination of him revealed he looked calm and rational."

"Your examination!? From across the street!? You gotta have 10-10 with an extra-long Stethoscope.

Five stories up!? He's on a ledge! five stories up. And he's Rational?"

"As I Said, he had been on the ledge 20 minutes already and procedure will not allow me to treat a Subject until I have final authorization. Such action would open the City up to law suits, Malpractice etc."

"Who the hell is going to Sue?"

"The Jumper of course."

He frowned, more like a pout. "I had been looking forward to a Nathan's all morning. My rationale was. Fifteen minutes. He'll be here when I get back. Pointing. And he is!! Doctor Leapoffski says ...."

I interrupted him. "NATHAN'S! That's in BROOKLYN! Coney Island! You went from here, Manhattan, to Coney Island in Brooklyn for a Hot Dog!? Leaving a jumper on a ledge!?"

"Like I said after 15 minutes, he wasn't going anywhere."

"Nathan's! You went all the way to Nathan's, Coney Island for a Hot Dog?

"You can get Nathan's right here in Manhattan, they sell them everywhere now." "Not the same. If you want 'Nathan's' you have to go to Coney Island.

It's the atmosphere, the ambience. And it isn't just HOT DOGS!"

Again the young guy didn't try to hide the contempt in his voice. Wagging his finger. "You! Just like all New Yorkers. You go to Nathan's only for the Dogs. The Hamburgers are great too. The corn on the cob, kissing his finger tips, and so is the cheesecake. I brought a piece of cheesecake back with me for dessert."

Squinting. "You got a jumper on a ledge waiting for you to come back from lunch, and you bring back dessert?"

"That's right and this time I'm gonna hide it. This Jumper won't get half." He bent down to pick up the bag he had dropped.

There was a sudden hushed groan mixed with screams from the Onlookers. The young man stood, "What happened?" "He Jumped."

The young man's eyes opened, he pursed his lips. Wagged his head. "Oh well, these thing happen."

I'm angry. "What happened to Doctor Leapoffski's 15 minute absolute no jump guarantee?"

He ever so slightly shook his head giving me a measured look. In all seriousness said. "He, that Jumper was predisposed. He violated Doctor Leapoffski's doctrine. Chapter 13, article 3 clearly states the 15 minute rule, plus or minus some time to adjust for the Subjects internal clock."

"What!!!! What's this Plus or Minus crap? You didn't mention Plus or Minus before."

He replied in the same superior tone. "There is always a Plus or Minus factor in all Science. Nothing is Absolute, Chapter 13 Article 3 clearly states."

I interrupted him again. "That plus or minus crap must be in Russian Standard Time." "I think there's an eight hour difference between here and Russia. Better call Olga, tell her to incorporate a Time Zone delay. Also tell her about the Jet Stream in case she decides to fly her broom over here for the wake."

The young man was holding the Cheesecake Bag at arm's length. "Someone stepped on it."

"Shouldn't you be over there?" I motioned with my head toward where the Jumper had fallen. "To Assist the Police."

"Nah, too messy. The EMS, Morgue and Police can take care of it. My work here is done. You can't win them all."

"Not if you don't try."

He ignored me, busy dropping the cheesecake bag in a trash can which surprisingly for NYC was not overflowing.

We watched as the people silently disperse heading for Subways and Buses.

Looking at his watch my Psych friend said. "Too late to go back to the Office. What say you to a piece of Danish? Cheesecake, much too heavy at this time of day. With a smile, but Danish would be just right."

I said, "Why not." I had just witnessed the death of a fellow man. 'No man is an island' etc. What better way to follow it than with a piece of Danish. Maybe I can get it Alamode.

"By the way, I asked. What's your name?"

"Peter, Peter Bureaucracatidus. It's from the Greek, meaning Large Maze. My ancestors in ancient Greece propose building a huge Maze in the Highway. A labyrinth to confuse invading enemies. The project was abandon because the Maze also confused friends. All was not lost however. Politicians even today are adopting the basic Maze Principle in reverse to expedite and simplify government.

Being used by the IRS and DMV. My ancestors, and still today have always been political. In the service of the people."

I visualized Archimedes running nude from the Baths thru the MAZE, lost, yelling "Eureka!" I have found IT!"

Peter's ancestors probably didn't know "IT" was lost.

Peter said with an engaging smile. "For Danish, we go up town." Finger pointing up. We walked a short distance to the Subway Entrance listening to the People talk.

I could hear two middle-aged women discussing the ordeal they had just witnessed. "Did you see him flapping his arms on the way down?" "Yeah, probably changed his mind. Dumb bastard! Only thinking of himself!" "His poor family. They're stuck with the bills. The Insurance! The insurance will never pay off."

"And his kids, if he had any. They are the ones who will suffer. The poor little ones will suffer for life. My heart goes out to them." "Talking about babies, Did you hear about Becky?" "Becky Rooney?" "Yes, she's pregnant again. Poor women. Married to that big lazy Irish Bum, sleeps all day." The other women quick to reply, "He's night bartender at the Waldorf, he has to sleep all day." "I don't care, the only thing he does is knock up poor Becky. He ought to be hung!" "I think he is hung."

The lady's conversation was powered out by two tough looking hard hats almost shouting at each other. "That bastard! If you're gonna jump, go off a bridge into the water. Shark Bait. Who the hell cares, cost me a day's work." A second voice, "Tied up the whole F'en City. I had to renew my driver's license, they closed the

F'en office. "You guys think you have problems" came a third voice. "I'm here to pay a fine for unused ash trays."

"Unused ashtrays?" "Yeah, I own a Restaurant up town. The Mayors Gestapo found three unused ash trays in my desk draw when they raided my restaurant at two AM."

"The Anti-Smoking League in their Brown Shirts and black SS Arm Bands gave me an ultimatum. I have to pay the fine otherwise my grandparents in their Rest Home will be terrorized."

"SS? What SS?" "Yeah, you know. SS. Stop Smoken." "When the smoke clears there will be no survivors. They're gonna start shipping everyone to Guantanamo."

"I understand the Ex Mayor smoked marijuana." "Used to, he quit, stunted his growth. He wears lifts."

"Did you hear about the new Cigarettes coming out?

They're in a Black Box with a White Skull and Cross Bones on it, like a Pirates Flag. They're called, "Jolly Roger." They have no tobacco but a proscribed amount of Marijuana for medical purposes." "No foolen!?" "Yeah, Honest to God! And the Anti-Smoking League is all for them. Just as long as non-smokers don't get a free Buzz inhaling their exhales. The Mayor has decreed that special non-smoking areas will be established in all Public Places for non-smokers."

"I thought you said they're for Medical purposes." "I did, Pointing to his head. All those F'en Anti-Smokers are sick. They're the same ones who want to legalize Marijuana." "Yeah, they say marijuana is healthy, good for you. Not habit forming, no more cancer, smoke e'm anywhere."

"Mayor deLate is all for these new smokes. He's on record. Before he's Through everybody in the city will have to smoke e'm. Forget the patch he says. Makes for a much happier City. No more crime. Get rid of the Police Force."

One of the Hard Hats stopped a Vendor pushing an Ice Cream Cart. Before he could ask the Vendor hollered back.

"All sold out!" "Everybody's sold out, Hot Dog Guy, everybody, even the Pretzel Guy." Yelling. "A jumper! good for business. They should have a "Jumper" once a week! All they gotta do is release a Looney from the Bin. Give e'm cab fare downtown. I'm gonna suggest it to the Mayor on his radio program. Think of the Taxes he could invent, maybe re-open the Firehouses." Another Hard Hat came right back. "Yeah, if he don't wanna do it maybe New Jersey will. Hell, everything's moving across the river. They own the Giants and Jets, Wall Street is next."

"New Jersey? I don't know. You got to take the Tunnel, the Bridge is closed."

I tried to visualize people licking Ice Cream Cones, eating Hot Dogs and Pretzels. Waiting to see a Man jump to his death from the fifth floor.

Easy way to do lunch when you don't want to miss the action. No matter which side of the Hudson you're on.

At the Subway Entrance, Mom and Pop Bangladesh with two young teenagers selling souvenir T-*Shirts*.

A young girl holding up a Shirt showing the figure of a man falling with the outline of a building in the background. "I SAW THE BIG JUMP."

People bunched up buying them. "American Enterprise."

Waiting for a train on the crowded Subway platform. Peter on his cell phone. "Important business."

Two large black guys standing nearby dressed in dark slacks and tastefully colorful shirts discussing the Jumper. They could easily be profiled as pushers especially when one smiled exposing a gold rimmed tooth.

"Never see our Black Brothers standing out on no ledge."

"No, that's just for white Dudes, something wrong with their Genes. It's a weakness." The smaller one said, "I hope He was straight with God." "Amen brother."

The voices faded. We boarded the uptown express for Danishville. Neither one of us got a seat. I realized I had been standing a long time. It was quiet in the train. All the passengers looking into their own inner distance. All witness to a human tragedy.

The stories they will tell tonight. The embellishments.

All to be forgotten in a day or two except for the Hot-Dog indigestion. I looked at a smiling Peter. Life goes on.

Introduction

"Repentant Scout"

"On my honor I will do my best……………….."

A Boy Scout is honest, truthful, plays by the rules.
I'm afraid I didn't meet all those attributes, to my
shame.

"Repentant Scout"

I never was a joiner or a follower. As a child or adult. By that I mean I never belonged to any Clubs, Fraternities or Political Parties etc. Oh, I'm a member in good standing with my Church. I don't belong to any Groups within the Church.

As for being a joiner, I did enlist in the military. I was too young for World War II but just right for Korea. With pride. Four years.

The reason I bring this up is, I just opened a tin box, actually a round tin container. This container once held a Fruitcake.

While in the service a long time ago my family sent me a Christmas Fruitcake. It came in the Tin Container I now hold in my hands.

After my buddies and I ate the cake I used the empty Tin to store knick- knacks.

The Tin became part of my gear and went with me whenever I moved. I brought the Fruitcake Tin home with me to my Mother and Fathers apartment when I was discharged from the Service. I lost track of it soon after I arrived home some sixty years ago.

The Fruitcake Tin was one of the items that came with my Mothers belongings after she passed away.

My Father had predeceased her. I put the Tin in the attic with the rest of my Mothers belongings.

The Fruitcake Tin was ignored for years. Well, not really ignored. It was too hard to open. I tried to open it a few times but the lid didn't want to come off. It required digging the fingernails into the edge and prying. It wouldn't move. All my tools were in the basement. I was too lazy to get them.

Curiosity was the only reason I had to open it. I was short on patience so I gave up.

The Tin sat pretty much where it had been put the day it arrived. I was in the attic this morning and came across the Tin.

I'm older now, 85. My curiosity pushed me. After a struggle, with the aid of tools and WD40 I opened the Tin.

I wish I could tell you I found a million dollars or a treasure map.

I didn't. Instead I found valueless coins I brought home from overseas, my old ID bracelet, dog tags and some uniform insignia.

I also found a Boy Scout Membership Dues Account Book, in my name. The book was still in its sleeve, brand new, unused.

I held the book in my hands and warmly remembered its origin. What it was doing in the Fruitcake Tin is a mystery.

The book resembles a Bank Savings Account Book. It had no entries.

I had paid no dues. I had attended no meetings. Except for my name and a number it was blank.

I make that point because it is important to the story.

Looking at the Book, a flood memories surfaced I didn't know were there. With a smile I close my eyes. I can feel and see the events that happen to me on a warm summer afternoon, when I was thirteen. Thoughts of a FRIDAY evening more than seventy years ago.

Let me tell you, The Saga of a Boy Scout Membership Book.

I grew up in New York City.

There were a few kids my age in the Neighborhood who were Boy Scouts. They were my friends. On some Friday evenings I would see them go to Scout meetings in their uniforms and occasionally hear them talk about Boy Scout Camp. Truthfully I never gave it a second thought. Occasionally they would tell me about their meetings and Scouting Activities. They were happy and enthusiastic. I never had a desire to be Boy Scout.

As I then understood, and I believe it's still the true today.

A Scout can earn an Award, called Merit Badge, for successfully completing Specialize Studies and or Tasks.

One of the neighborhood Scouts lived in the same Apartment Building as me.

His name was Jerry. He explained that he would get a Merit Badge if he could get a kid to sign up, become a Boy Scout.

I said no. Truthfully, even if I wanted to become a Scout. My family could not afford it. The uniform itself was too expensive.

He kept after me, asking almost every day. It got to where he was pest, pleading with me. All I had to do, he said, was to pass the Boy Scout Test. No! He kept pestering me.

Then he hit a nerve. He implied I was not smart enough to pass the test. I fumed. He wasn't that smart to imply it just to get me to join.

He did not know, he had challenged me. The gauntlet had been thrown.

I said, "OK." He darn near jumped for joy.

I barrowed his Boy Scout Hand Book. He showed me what I had to know to pass the test.

I went off by myself to study. Tied the knots with a piece of old clothes line, the Sheepshank was the hardest. I memorized the Pledge and whatever else was required.

I forget how long it took but I finished pretty fast. I remember reviewing the information waiting for to Gerry come back.

"What's next?" I asked.

He said I would have to be tested by the Scoutmaster. I wanted to get it done.

Jerry said the Scoutmaster lives in the neighborhood.

Maybe he's home. I was pumped up. "Let's go." I intimidated him.

I think about that now. Today we'd just pick up a phone, call the Scoutmaster for an appointment. But in those days most households didn't have telephones and if they did kids were not allowed to use them.

We walked about four blocks to the Scoutmasters Home. All the way Gerry kept asking me if I was sure I could pass. He didn't think I had studied long enough. I think he felt that if I failed it would reflect on him.

We got to the Scoutmasters house and after some prodding Jerry went up the steps and rang the bell. I stayed on the sidewalk. I saw Jerry talking to a man in the doorway. Jerry turned and pointed to me. The man step out onto the porch and beckoned me to come up. I didn't like it but I went.

The man was tall with gray hair. He stooped a little and took my hand. He introduced himself.

I never met the man before or seen him since but I still remember his name. Mr. Bone. I'm not sure of the spelling. He was the Scoutmaster.

He sent Jerry to the other end of the long porch so he could not hear us. Then he and I sat and we talked.

He asked about my family, sports and school. He made it sound like school was fun. I don't know how he got that idea, but he was a nice old guy.

He had a quiet reassuring voice, easy to talk to. He never asked me why I wanted to become a Scout.

Even sitting down his height made me feel small.

Answering his questions I remembered thinking I wasn't very interesting but I guess he was satisfied because he gave me Scout Test, knots and all.

I passed. The Scoutmaster congratulated me, shook my hand. I remember feeling good because he was pleased.

I think back now and the only word that I can think to describe him is Gracious. He had to be. To have two kids ring his door bell, unannounced. To welcome us and to take time to treat us as if we were important, that's Grace. What really impressed me was it was easy to see he was really pleased we were there. No wonder I still remember the man and his name.

Jerry was very happy I passed. He was going to get his Merit Badge.

On the way home I was feeling relieved. Jerry talked non-stop about the Scouts. That's when I found out it was Friday.

Jerry informed me this is Friday, Scout night. Meeting night. Tonight! would be my first Scout Meeting.

That's why even to this day I remember it all happened on a Friday.

I didn't panic but I could feel panic churning, wanting to get loose.

How do I get out of this? It was going too fast for me. One minute I was me the next minute I was a Boy Scout.

I had past the Boy Scout Test but I never intended to be a Scout. I never considered going to meetings.

Walking home after the Scout test I was only partially listening to Jerry. My mind was in denial. How do I get out of this?

That's when I heard Jerry say, "We."

Another surprise. By "We" he meant all the neighborhood Scouts get together and walk to the meeting together, as a group. I didn't like it. Feeling trapped. The Meeting! Too much! Too soon! I didn't want to go. I did my thing! I took the test! Enough! I just won't go!

Jerry was happy and animated. I didn't want to tell him I wasn't going to the meeting.

I told him I would meet him there. He pleaded with me to go with them, him and the other Scouts. I think he wanted to show me off as a trophy.

"OK" I lied just to shut him up. I hate to hear people plead.

I don't think he believed me because he said he would ring my doorbell. I remember thinking he was good at ringing doorbells.

Then I remembered my family didn't know I had joined the Scouts.

I told him I would meet him, "Out front." That's the front of our building.

My parents wouldn't care if I were a Boy Scout. I just did not want them to know. I didn't want anyone to know. I don't know why I felt that way.

I think I felt I was giving up part of me. My privacy. Whatever, I didn't like it. There are a lot of, "I didn't like it" in this story.

My first Boy Scout Meeting. Scout Meetings were held in the basement of the Church Institute.

The institute was an impressive old style two story stone building with columns and steps in front. I had never been inside.

Jerry and I met four other Scouts one block over from where we lived. I knew all of them and we were friends. I didn't know them as a Scout and that seemed to make a difference.

They were in their Boy Scout Uniforms. They looked so clean.

I was in my street clothes. The same clothes I had worn that afternoon taking the Test. The same clothes I put on clean that morning. I didn't feel comfortable.

Till that time I had never been aware of my appearance. I didn't like it. Jerry told the other Scouts how I had studied for the Test about an hour and how we walked over to the Scoutmasters house. That I passed the Test with no trouble and the Scoutmaster was impressed.

That set them all talking. A lot of "Wow's."

At the institute we went down two flights of steps to a finished basement. A double set of doors open to a gymnasium size room with exercise equipment on two walls. Doors were open to three smaller but large size rooms. The rooms were clean and well lit with old style ceiling lights.

Lots of Scouts were there, all in uniform. They were talking, laughing, running around having fun. The guys I came with mixed in with their friends so I was alone.

I did catch some looks. I leaned against a wall and watched.

Didn't seem orderly to me. There were no adults present. Leaning on the wall tired of waiting. I really didn't want to there. I remember getting ready to leave. All I had to do was ease over to the door I came in, then I'm gone. Just then two men in Scout Uniforms came in through my exit door.

I found out they were Assistant Scoutmasters and they ran the meetings. The Scoutmaster I had seen that afternoon wasn't going to be there.

I didn't like it. The two Assistant called for order and got the Scouts attention. "Fall In." As I watched everyone silently went to different places in the room and lined up. Attendance was taken and some other business. Everyone got busy doing something and it was quiet.

I stood out like a leaky fire hydrant. One foot up leaning back against the wall in street clothes hands in my pockets. Maybe I could still escape.

I saw Jerry talking to one of the Assistants and pointing to me. Too late they got me.

The Assistant came over and introduced himself. We went into one of the rooms where he had a desk. He welcomed me and we talked.

He was not the same caliber as the Scoutmaster I had met that afternoon. He didn't inspire the same closeness and trust but he was friendly. An authoritative figure. He took the same information I had given the Scoutmaster that afternoon when I took the test. He recorded it. After he got all my information he explained that the Scouts are divided into Troupes. The Troupes are divided into Patrols and I was being assigned to a new Patrol that was just forming. The Beaver Patrol. He told me the Beaver Patrol was composed of new Scouts so, "You should feel right at home." He introduced me to the members of the Beaver Patrol and, "The Patrol leader." They were all SHRIMPS, little Kids, looked like they just graduated from the Cub Scouts. It should have been called the Peewee Patrol. I didn't like it. The Patrol Leader, was older and bigger about my size.

The Patrol Leader was explaining something to me when a whistle blew. Activity time started. Something was going to happen. Each Patrol was matched against another Patrol to do something. Tug of War!

The Patrols were going to have Tugs of War till one Patrol won.

I was strong. I liked Tugs of War. The Beaver Patrol was pitted against the Stag Patrol.

The Stag Patrol lined up at one end of the rope. I looked at the Stags. They were all bigger than me. Me and the Patrol Leader were the biggest Guys on the Beaver side.

I wanted to yell foul but I was a new guy so I kept my mouth shut.

The Beaver Patrol, looked so out match that all the other Patrols stopped to watch us loose.

I did not understand why the Assistants allow this to happen. So much for Fair Play I thought.

We lined up. The mighty Beavers against the Stags. I was the last one on the rope. I told the Beavers to stand sideways plant their feet stay low and pull. Ready Set Go! We never had the chance. The Stags pulled and the Beavers started to slide. I had to hand it to the little guys they were really trying.

The Stags weren't even giving it their best. Fact is some were just laughing. Really made me mad and I pulled as hard as I could. We, the Beavers were Being pulled, sliding on the wood floor to the foul line.

Just then I was sliding past a doorknob. I looped the rope around the knob. The sliding stopped.

The Stags were surprised. They pulled harder, they pulled and pulled. All the laughing stopped. The little Beavers really thought they had stopped the Stags.

I was crotched sideways in front of the knob, making believe I was pulling hard so no one could see the rope looped around the knob.

All the other Scouts stopped to watch the Stags pull and the Beavers hold. Now everyone cheering for the Beavers. The Stags pulled with all their might.

That's when I realized it was wrong. Didn't know what to do. I let rope slip off the knob.

CRASH!!!!! The Stags when backwards tumbling over each other. There were legs, arms and bodies all tangled up rolling on the floor banging into each other. The other Scouts had to jump to get out of the way. It was over, the Stags picking themselves up. A mess.

The Beavers had stumbled backward but never really fell down. They stood there stunned, bewildered. Didn't realized what had happened. No one did. The Beavers were just little guys. They heard and saw the other Patrols laughing so they laughed too. That made the Stags mad. It looked to them like the Beavers had let go of the rope.

In a way it was funny. Seeing the Stags laying on the floor all jumbled up red faced with embarrassment and fury. Little Beavers standing there laughing. The Stags were mad and probably would have hurt the Beavers but the two Assistants finally intervened.

I was standing up front. If the Stags wanted to hurt the Peewee's they would have to go through me and this time I had no Knobs to help me. I'm sure I would have got the worst of it.

I didn't mean for it to happen the way it did. But once I looped the knob I was committed. No way out. Dumb thing for a kid to do.

The Assistant I had talked to earlier asked me to step outside with him. He had seen the whole thing. I was a Knob Looper.

He took me out front and we sat on the steps. He was very serious. He said a Scout is honest, truthful and doesn't cheat. He lectured me about Scout Hood and fair play. That, those boys, the Stags, could have been hurt. He was right. I didn't mention how unfair the Tug of War was. I meekly agreed, bobbing my head to everything he said. I knew it before he said it. I had just studied it all for my test that afternoon. He repeated himself more than once. Like a long sermon in church that seems to go on and on and you can't leave.

I just wanted him to finish. He did a good job.

Finally, he look into my eyes. I had trouble holding his gaze. I kept wanting to blink.

He said that I should sit out here on the steps for a while, think about what we had just discussed and then come back inside. He stood, momentarily looked down at me and left.

I waited a minute or two, looked around the corner to make sure he was gone. I left, never to come back. All the way home I was happy. Felt like I had just escaped a dreaded confinement.

Two, three weeks later the Scout Membership Book came in the mail. The same one I now hold in my hand. I remember looking at the Book when it arrived. I truly valued the book. I put the book away some place safe, never to see it again till just now. Over 70 years.

I don't know how the Book got into the Fruit Cake Tin. Perhaps my Mother put it there. But if I had trouble opening the Tin. How did she? Maybe it is the spirit of that Scoutmaster from a long time ago telling me my Account is still open and I owe the Scouts something.

Epilogue;

—⊗⊗—

"The Repentant Scout"

I am still who I am and the Boy Scouts thank God are still who they are. The Scouts will always be my favorites. That's why my son, who is now a Father of three young adults, was a Boy Scout when he was a boy. I drove him to his meetings on Friday nights. His Sons were also Scouts.

I'm 85 years old now. Looking at life backwards through the long tunnel of time I see things a little different. Also my brain has slowed down, not so eager to rush to judgment. I would like to think now that the Assistant Scoutmasters in this story told the bigger boys in the Stag Patrol to take it easy on the little Beavers. Make the Beavers feel like they were in the game so the Beavers would not feel left out. And it was only after the door knob interred the game and the laughter of the other Patrols that the Stags felt challenged and Pulled Hard. It was only a thirteen year old, me, finding fault with something he wanted to find fault with that tinted the game. Now, with a sense of guilt, looking thru my tunnel, holding the Scout Book in my hand, remembering a Friday evening a long time ago. I can say, with sincerity, sorry Stags.

Introduction

"Nathan's"

Nathan's, No Napkins.

"Nathan's"

I'm 85 years old. When I speak of the past, big events become "Moments." Let me tell you a story, a happy "Moment" I still remember. Oh, I've had an abundance of happy Moments in my life but this one is really special, one of the earliest. Still fresh in my mind.

I was born in New York City, 1930, the great depression. We didn't have much, times were tough. I remember having my first Nathan's hot dog.

I was just a little boy. I remember because it was a wonderful treat when you didn't have many treats. I remember because I was hungry and it tasted great. The flavor of that Nathan's dog lasted years. Impacted my memory where I could actually taste my memory.

Nathan's, an open air Hot Dog Stand located in Coney Island, Brooklyn.

Brooklyn is located on Long Island in New York City.

In the summer of 1941 I lived in Queens also located on Long Island. So Brooklyn and Queens are neighbors. Not as close as it sounds.

In 1941 I was 11 years old. I had been selling deposit bottles, delivering orders, different odd jobs, working for pennies. I did this to make money, but spent it as fast as I made it. Penny candy etc. It was not as lucrative as it sounds.

This time I saved my earnings. Took months. I think it amounted to about twenty five cents. I protected that money like Fort Knox. Really there was no place to hide it. My corrupt older brother would find it. Burning a hole in my pocket. I decided I would spend it.

After careful consideration I decided I would go to Coney Island for Nathan's. NYC in those days when you said "Nathan's" everyone knew you meant "Hot Dog."

Nathan's, A special Hot Dog. The only place you could get a Nathan's in 1941 was Coney Island.

As a ten, eleven year old I had gone to Coney by myself several times. Never told any adults.

The elevated subway train was located a block away from where I lived in Queens. The subway cost a nickel. A nickel was a lot of money. No body jumped turnstiles in those days. We were a law abiding bunch back then. I did not have a nickel.

Waiting on the first deck of the train elevator I could tell by the sound of an incoming train where it was on the track. Just at the right sound I would rush around the corner under the turnstile up to the top deck and on the train just as the door was closing. Happy to tell you it worked every time. I was a clever little rascal. None of my friends would try it. Did I say no one jumped the turnstiles?

(Under it). I would take the IRT train all the way to Stillwell Ave, Coney Island, Brooklyn.

If I remember, over an hour ride. I used to go to Coney with no money. Spend the day looking at the amusements, the people, walk the Boardwalk and the beach.

I'd always stop to look and smell Nathan's. All day on an empty stomach. I loved it. Sneak back on the subway going home, under the turnstile hidden in the Coney crowd. Always an adventure.

Excited! Today's the day. I'm going to Coney to buy a Nathan's. Waiting on the train elevator, listening to the sound. There it is. Run! under the turnstile, up the stairs to the closing doors. Out of breath, I made it. On the train, long ride. Going to Coney. This time with money.

The closer I got to Coney the more anxious I became. Hand in my pocket fingering my coins, Rich. Summoning up all my courage. I went to Nathan's. Stood in line with all the big people. Looking up at the counter man, real loud! "I want a Hot Dog. I want it loaded with sauerkraut with lots of mustard." The counterman made me my dog, bare handed, no gloves required then. "You want something to drink?" Drink? Never thought. "Ok, Ok, I'll take a Root beer." "That will be twenty cents." Reaching up over the tall counter. The Counter man placed a dog piled high with kraut, oozing mustard into my little hand. An over flowing Root Beer in the other hand. Standing there, looking at them, overpowered me. Mustard and kraut squeezing and falling on my hand, Root Beer dripping. Holding them out in front of me, walking, looking for a place to sit, Careful! Careful!

I found a seat. Relieved. God I was happy. Holding the dog up in my hand, looking at it. Dog sticking out of both ends. Mustard oozing, kraut piled high, too high for my mouth, a dream come true. "Thanks God."

I opened my mouth as wide as I could. 'Bite top to bottom! Top to bottom! Small bites! Small bites.' Mustard, kraut all over my face, hands. Cautioned myself, Chew! Chew! Make it last, enjoy the flavor, chew, that great Nathans flavor. Closed my eyes. Heaven.

The last bite, too soon. Looking at it. Reluctantly put it in my mouth. The last chew. Make it last!

Still remember the regret, swallowing.

Napkin? No way!! Scrap the Mustard and Kraut off my face, licked the Mustard and Kraut off my fingers. Fantastic!!! My dirty eleven year old hands licked clean, spotless, savoring the flavor. Wonderful!

85 years. Eleven years old. Still remember. A happy Moment. Hope you enjoyed it with me.

Nathan's Hot Dog, Bun, Mustard and Sauerkraut. All Nathan's. Unbeatable combination, a delight. I'll take two to go, when I go.

I've had many Nathan's since then, each better than the last.

Nathan's. 100 Years old. A national treasure. My suggestion to all NYC visitors.

1. Visit the Statue of Liberty. A spiritual obligation. Also see the Statue at night on the Staten Island Ferry. On deck. Right side

going left returning. Fantastic! The Ferry is free on Sunday. Bring a camera.

2. Visit the Empire State Building. All the Museums, Broadway, Parks etc. Then, Go to Nathan's, Coney Island. Go Hungry. Have a Dog. Lots of Mustard and Sauerkraut, maybe a Root Beer. A happy moment you will remember the rest of your days.

Bon-Appetite

Introduction

"A Tree that Falls"

A Tree grows. Like so many mysteries in life no one knows if trees can communicate.

A life time of silence.

Like a swan. Should a tree be allowed to make a sound when it falls?

"A Tree that Falls"

One evening I attended a social gathering at a neighbor's home.

The other guests attending where from different backgrounds, all opinionated making for lively discussions. The conversations in the room, Political and Social were at times intense. But always cordial.

Too early in the evening the conversation hit a lull. The Hostess replenishing every ones drink dutifully tried to restart the conversation with minimal success.

In the awkward silence, she looked at me and said, "John, if a tree falls in a forest and no one is there to hear it. Does it make a sound?"

This question she hoped would bridge the lull. She addressed the question to me. I was on the spot. I looked at the other faces in the room. All intent. I could have shrugged my shoulders, "I don't know?" I didn't.

A tree falling is a popular question and seems to astound everyone. The question has taken on a life of its own. Whoever first posed the question is still laughing. I am an Engineer. The answer for me is academic.

On my second drink. Gin and Tonic. I drink for Medicinal purpose only. The Tonic is good for leg cramps.

Academic? How do I poise my answer? Standing, center of the room. Looking at everyone. How to keep their interest?

'Make it sound like a mystery.' Looking at the Guests from under my eye brows.

Stooped down. Low questioning voice, "If a tree falls in a forest and no one is there to hear it, does it make a Sound?" Smiles. I had their attention. With an equally low mystical voice looking at all of them. "Picture this." Spreading my arms. "A magnificent tree stands in the middle of a forest. It stands alone in its own meadow, the tallest of trees, fully formed, rich green bows, beautifully shaped. Majestically it stands, looking at God all day, its branches raised in adoration." Everyone's attention. Smiling.

"This tree represents many things. It provides a home for birds, squirrels, all sorts of other Creatures.

To the Lumber Jack, the tree, timber to be cut down. To a Poet, a place to dream, to compose. To a Hiker, a place to rest, to nap. To an Artist, a beautiful vista for a blank canvas, never to fully capture its Grandeur. To an Engineer? Shrugging, the tree is all of those things. But an Engineer, dead beat that he is, reduces everything to basics. An Engineer sees in the tree a great source of energy. Energy that lives in the tree because of its great height and weight.

This energy is called, Momentum. Momentum." Twisting my head to see everyone. "Momentum is easy to understand." Swishing my empty glass quickly through the air, "Simply put, the faster a weight moves the more Momentum it has. And momentum is Energy."

Handing my empty glass out to the Hostess. Leg cramps.

Looking under my brows. "Now we go back to the tree. Visualize the tree. It is very tall. It is very heavy. For some unknown reason this magnificent tree is suddenly uprooted. It topples and starts to fall."

"Back to Momentum!"

"The tree falls. Its weight falls, faster and faster."

"Remember, Momentum equals how fast a weight moves, Falls." As the tree falls faster and faster the Momentum increases, grows and grows. Remember, Momentum is Energy. As the Momentum increases so does the Energy." Suddenly! Slamming my hand down on a table top.

BANG! Everyone, wide eyed! Got their attention!

"The tree slams onto the ground! Releasing a tremendous amount of built up Momentum, Energy."

Holding up my palms, questioning look. "That Energy Has To Go Some Place!! Some of the energy is absorbed by the ground. But the ground can't absorb all the Energy quickly enough so the tree actually bounces, the unabsorbed Energy pushing it back."

Scary voice again, fingertips fluttering, "This unabsorbed Energy is transferred to the air as Energy Waves. These Energy Waves have no sound. They travel soundlessly, finger tips still fluttering, "Soundlessly," through the forest until all their energy is spent."

"If a person happens to be standing nearby when the tree slams into the ground, the unabsorbed energy waves will strike that persons ear drum. The ear drum will vibrate. The brain will interrupt those vibrations as noise, sound.

If the ear drum is absent there is no sound."

"A tree falls in a forest. Does it make a sound?

"Only if you are there to hear it."

"A tree falls, only Gods other Creatures in the forest are there to hear the noise whatever that noise sounds like to them. "Thus, if a man is in a forest alone, without his wife, and he speaks, is he still wrong?"

Note; The Physics of the falling tree and its impact are much more complex than described but the basics are there.

The Social Gathering at my neighbor's house that evening, after a few more G and T's, was an echoing success. I am happy to report, the tree described in this story still stands, in my heart.

Introduction

"Lazarus"

Arise my dear Lazarus, the World awaits.

"The Death of Lazarus"

Jesus arrives four days after his friend Lazarus has died. Lazarus has already been buried.

Lazarus sister Martha is grief stricken.

Accusingly to Jesus, "If only you would have come earlier my brother would still be alive."

Jesus tries to console her but she is beyond consolation.

Finally Jesus tells the workmen to remove the stones from the cave entrance where Lazarus is entombed.

When the stones have been removed. Jesus stands a distance away from the opening and says in a loud commanding voice. "Lazarus come out." He repeats "Lazarus come forth!"

To every ones amazement Lazarus walks slowly out. He walks out dragging burial cloths and wrappings, one hand shielding his eyes from the sun.

He stops, majestically standing there, head raised, arms out, looks at his surroundings and yells out.

"JESUS H. CHRIST!!!" "Why did you bring me back here?

I was having a great time in Heaven playing Johnny ride the pony with Moses and the rest of the boys."

Jesus looks at Lazarus Sister, shrugs his shoulders, "You can't please everybody. He always was a pain in the ass."

"I'm going back to my shtick, Wine to Water routine." Lazarus sister, "Water to Wine."

"I don't know! I get confused."

"Is Murphy's still open?"

Introduction

"A Brief Moment"

A long trip through the perils of life.

From here to there.

Just a Brief Moment.

"A Brief Moment"

Clear winter day. I had just purchased a Christmas tree from a vendor across the street from a children's park. Tying the tree to the roof of my car. I couldn't help but notice what looked like an old man in an overcoat sitting on a swing in the park warring a knit hat. Best I could see he wasn't moving just sitting looking onto space.

Got the tree tied down securely. The Guy is still sitting there. Doesn't looked like he has moved.

I looked around, could see no car. How did he get there? Is he lost? How is he going to get home?

Got in my car. All I have to do is turn the key, start the engine and drive away. Let me explain. I'm not the kind of guy who gets involved.

Sitting there. I'm Christian. A week before Christmas. I don't get involved. I don't know what propelled me. But it felt secure once I got started.

I walked into the park to where the old guy was sitting. Gloved hands in his lap. "Waiting for someone to push you?" Looking up, hint of a smile. "Just reminiscing." Wrinkled forehead. "I'm 92 years old. I do a lot of reminiscing." "About what?" "Yesterday."

"I was passing this park with some other seniors when I saw this swing hanging here all by itself.

Oh! I'm with a group of seniors from the Center in town. We're here to see a tree lighting next block up." A little chuckle, "They don't know I'm missing." His voice, clear, wistful. Looking straight ahead.

"My grandfather use to take me to the park when I was a little boy. He would push me on the swing." A sigh, "Long time ago." Looking up at me. "He was a good man." Still looking, "A lot of good men and women back then." Tilting his head. "My memories are vague but I do remember being young." Eyes twinkling, "Being able to run, jump, walk without pain." Smiling. With a sigh. "Thoughtlessly young. There was always tomorrow," Eyes changing, taking on a distant look. "Young! Going to school." Looking up, "Oh! I wasn't best student. Didn't study much. Got in trouble with the teachers and such." Head tip. "Boyish mischief. Never hurt anyone." "Being young!" Shaking his head. "Young! Only once, once in a life time."

I sat down on the swing next to him. Listening. Cold on my seat.

"As a young man I worked hard and played hard. The War came. A pause. I served my country. Bad places. Bad memories. Still with me.

I married a wonderful girl, smiling looking up, pretty too!

Two beautiful children." Holding up two fingers. Looking at me, hurt in his eyes. "My Son. My Son was killed in another War." Quivering voice, "Broke my heart." Shaking his head. "In a moment's time. War kills individuals by thousands leaving loved ones a life time of grief."

"I lost my dear wife, the love of my life to her enlarged heart. Heart too big. She tried to embrace everyone."

"Cancer claimed my wonderful beautiful daughter, picture of her Mother." Lowing his head. "Why can't they find a cure?"

Looking up to the sky. Distant. "Christmas. We never had much to give. A sigh, But we always had lots of love." A thoughtful smile. "Christmas was the happiest time." Touching my arm. "This will be my last Christmas. Distance in his eyes. I am a God fearing man. I worked hard all my life. Loved and cared for my family. Always tried to do the right thing." Searching. "I have out lived my family, my relatives and my friends. I have no one." Mournfully, barely a whisper. "When I die, no one will know I was here." Silence.

"I'll know you were here Old Man."

"Thank you." Looking at me, deep, warm smile. "Let me wish you a Merry Christmas."

'Damn! I don't get involved.'

"Come on old man, I'll drive you home." Broad smile, eyes gleaming. "Just give me one push."

Have a Merry and Thoughtful Christmas.

Introduction

"End of the Road"

The direction is clear. No stops. Straight thru.

Eternity awaits.

Eternity, Such a long time.............

"End of the Road"

Saint Peter standing with God at the entrance to heaven.

Pete, mopping his brow, big red handkerchief, little green visor over his tired eyes.

Pete looks around shaking his head. It's been a busy day.

The Turnstiles haven't stopped turning all day as one lucky Soul after another is given a Token for the Up Turnstile and wave through to Paradise.

God to Peter, rubbing his hands, "We're doing great." Pete grins, "Yeah, Thursday's have always been good."

"Hate the weekends. Got to use both Elevators and Escalators DOWN, running full time, never stops." Peter's attention is caught by a Soul moving tentatively toward him holding his scroll of life. The Good Lord moves a little closer.

The Soul stops in front of Peter, shoulders down. Murmurs his name. Peter looks at soul and unrolls his Scroll of Life.

Peters tired eyes studies the Scroll.

All Red Entries. Not one Blue. "Oops," Hardly noticeable, there is one tiny Blue Entry at the bottom. Looking close, the lonely Blue

Entry states that at one time to impress his boss this soul reluctantly gave a Beggar a dime.

He did so only after his Boss had given the Beggar some coins. Other than that Dime the Soul had been a mean spirited bastard, deliberately causing much pain and suffering to those around him. No remorse.

Peter looks up from the Scroll shaking his head.

"Ahem." Murmurs the Lord. Peter turns to God saying, "You got enough to do! Let me handle this!"

"No, no, let me help." Peter shrugs. The Lord studies the Scroll.

Reaching out to Peter with compassion radiating love and forgiveness.

"He did give a Dime to a poor Beggar. A dime that helped the beggar in his time of need. An act of charity and kindness." Touching Peter's sleeve. The Lords eyes radiating love. "What should we do with him?"

Peter, Tilt of the head. Side of his mouth.

"Give him back his Dime, tell him to go to Hell!"

Introduction

"David"

Goliath, that big SOB. Intimidated the whole Jewish Army. David saved the day. The evening too.

"David"

"Are you kidding!? I'm not going up against that big Son-of-a-Bitch." "But you're the biggest guy in our army." "Get somebody else."

Goliath stands raging. Waving his sword. Yelling obscenities. Humiliating the whole reluctant Jewish Army. Having a ball.

"We got to get somebody!" "No volunteers!" "Grab Somebody! Anybody!" "Throw someone up there for that gorilla to tear apart so we can go home." "Sure would be a shame to mess up one of our new uniforms."

"We got this little Sheppard kid outside with a sling shot. Says he is not afraid of Goliath."

"Has he ever seen Goliath?" "Don't think so." "He don't have a new uniform." "That's a plus." "Put a blind fold on him and send him up there." "Good idea."

The battle is over. Goliath is dead. "Damn kid, you did a great job!" "Piece of cake." "You're pretty good with that sling shot." "It's all in the wrist." "Careful kid, swinging it around you gonna hurt somebody."

"Where you afraid facing Goliath?" "Are you kidding? When they took the blind fold off I shit my pants. It was running down my leg."

"Goliath say anything?" "That's some stink kid, burns my eyes." "That's when you got him?" "Yeah. His eyes were closed."

"What can we do for you as a reward?" "I got my eye on that little cutie in the corner. What's her name?" "Bathsheba." "I'll grab her."

"She's married to a General." "No problem, I'll get another stone."

Riding off on the General's horse, Bathsheba on his lap whispering in her ear. "Hang in with me Babe. I got a Godfather. He's going to make me king one day."

Introduction

"Grandma's house"

For all occasions,
Grandma's House is the safest place to be.

"Grandma's House"

Five year old Maggie lifts Cuddles out of her box. Cuddles, a tiny fluffy adorable little kitten. She is purring, "Hello Maggie."

Cuddles is in grave danger. Maggie has to save her. They have to get to Grandma's house.

"You better be quiet. They might find you." Maggie looks all around. There is danger everywhere. "We must get away." Maggie walks along the darkened hallway to the door. Cuddles following her.

Maggie opens the door and looks out onto the street. It is very dark. She can see no one. She is frightened looking back at Cuddles. "You have to stay close to me." Cuddles presses against her ankle.

Looking out on the dark street. "We have to go now." Maggie sneaks out onto the street. She hurries along stooped over staying very close to the buildings. Cuddles trying to keep up. Maggie stops. "Shush." Two big men in hoods, dark shadows carrying big sticks are on the street walking towards them. Maggie grabs Cuddles and runs into a dark alley.

Maggie crouches down holding Cuddles close in her arms. "Shush, don't make a sound." The menacing men look into the alley with their big sticks. Maggie can hear the Men grumbling. They sound mean. Maggie shaking crouching down. The Men do not see Maggie and Cuddles, they move on. Maggie knows there are other mean men looking for them. "Cuddles we have to be extra careful." She could hear Cuddles purring, "Yes we have to be careful.

"We have to get to Grandma's house before they find out your gone." They start down the dark street. Maggie praying they meet no more hooded men with big sticks.

Suddenly Cuddles runs away across the street to a door way and begins to meow at the door. Maggie is stunned, she calls out in a whisper, "Cuddles we have to go. The men with the big sticks will be coming. Cuddles meows all the louder calling out to her friend Poodles. She doesn't want to leave without saying goodbye to Poodles. The door opens and there's Poodles. A little fuzzy dog no bigger than Cuddles. Cuddles and Poodles playfully hugging each other Poodles licking Cuddles face.

"Cuddles we have to go!" Maggie tries to separate them. Poodles does not want Cuddles to go. Maggie hears a shout! "There they are!" Two dark hooded men with sticks are running down the street.

Maggie grabs Cuddles and runs around the corner into a dark doorway and hides. Two men with big sticks come around the corner looking for them. Maggie can hear the men grumbling as they search all the door ways. They're grumbling getting louder poking their sticks as they are come closer to Maggie's hiding place. It is very dark. Maggie is scared. She climbs up onto the highest step with Cuddles. Holding Cuddles in her arms. "Keep quiet Cuddles don't make a sound." Big dark shadows of the men in their hoods come to Maggie's door way. They are looking, poking their sticks in the doorway trying to find Maggie. Maggie can hear the men grumbling louder and louder. Their grumblings make Maggie shiver, they sound so mean. Their sticks are poking close. Maggie squeezes herself small holding Cuddles close, she is shaking. Maggie's heart is pounding. She can hear the stick coming closer. She holds her breath clutches Cuddles, eyes closed tight. The stick right next to her. She can hear it. Almost touching. The stick misses her. The men grumble louder and go away. Cuddles jumps down and scoots away out of the doorway. Maggie running after her.

Cuddles darts back and forth in front of Maggie. She is playing.

Maggie can't catch her. Maggie looking for the men with the sticks.

She is anxious and frightened trying to capture Cuddles. "Cuddles there is danger everywhere. The men with the sticks will be back and get us.

We must be going." Cuddles comes to her purring. "I'm sorry."

"No use trying to make amends. We might get caught because of you." Maggie and Cuddles dart down the street looking in every direction. Finally, there it is! Grandma's house! Right in front of them. Looking at Cuddles.

"We have to get to Grandma's house to be safe." Maggie is happy. She scoops up Cuddles and they Run! Run, Run, to Grandma's House. Maggie suddenly stops, clutching Cuddles in her arms fear in her heart. Two big hooded men with sticks standing in front of Grandmas house. Maggie, scared, did the Men see them? They have to hide. Maggie and Cuddles quickly hide from the two Men.

They are not safe. Maggie holds Cuddles close. They can hear the other Men from Town coming closer. They are not safe! Maggie holds Cuddles close. What are they to do?

The Men in front of Grandma's House are very big and look very dangerous. They are wearing dark hoods over their heads with long black robes. In the shadows Maggie can see other Men searching in all directions waving their big sticks. Maggie has never been so frightened, trembling holding Cuddles close.

Maggie and Cuddles must get inside Grandma's house to be safe.

They can hear the other men coming to get them. They're getting closer. What are Maggie and Cuddles to do!? Maggie sees Grandma open her front door. "No no, Grandma don't go outside." She is frightened for Grandma. "Those big Men with their big sticks will get you." She wants to shout! "Grandma, don't go out!" What will they do to poor little Grandma???? I'll close my eyes! Maggie sees Grandma storming out of her house holding a broom over her head. She strides right up to the Big Bad Hooded Men.

Swinging her broom. SURPRISE!!! Maggie can't believe her eyes. The big men turn and ran away taking the other bad men with them. Maggie joyfully holding Cuddles runs to Grandma shouting.

"Grandma! Grandma! You chased them away, you chased them away!!!

Grandma hugging Maggie and Cuddles, "You're safe now." "Grandma, you chased them away! How did you do it?" Grandma raised her broom, a big smile.

"Nobody messes with Grandma!" Cuddles climbing into Grandmas arms, Maggie said, "I love you Grandma."

PS You're always safe in Grandma's house.

Introduction

"Deep Water"

Story of a young Kid making
a decision beyond him.

"Deep Water"

Some mysteries are made to be unsolved.

An unsolved mystery has haunted me for a lifetime.

There was six of us, great friends. The year was 1947. We were 16, 17.

Eddy was the biggest, over six feet. He was a brainy, delightful guy, a free spirit. His father owned a gas station garage. Eddy worked repairing cars, Engines. A great natural mechanic. All he ever wanted to do.

He quit High School even though he was above average. Went on to become a successful business man in later life.

Got a driver's license illegally at an early age. Eddy purchased a 1931 Buick 8 passenger automobile. I call it "Automobile" instead of car because it was BIG, Huge. No dents, no scratches. Wooden spoke wheels. Spares mounted either side in the front fenders. Two fold down seats in the back to accommodate 5 rear passengers. We felt like gangsters riding in that car. It had a personality. The fun we had in that car even today remembered was awesome. We'd pile in and take off for places we'd never go if it weren't for Eddy and "The Hotel Buick", the car's nick name. We did sleep in it on occasion.

The "Hotel Buick", we had a lot of affection for that car.

Six to eight laughing guys piling out of that car. We were a sensation where ever we landed.

We were still in High School. Eddy worked, covered the expenses where ever we went.

This story starts on a hot Saturday morning. Eddy drove us in the Hotel Buick to a small public beach out on long Island.

A couple guys were with us who weren't part of our group. We knew them. They were welcome. It was always a treat for anyone to go with us.

The beach was nice, we had never been there before. Looking across a channel we could see a Gated Community Private Beach with Sliding Pons and other action toys. Very inviting. Some of the guys, real strong swimmers, decided they would swim across.

I'm not a strong swimmer. I gaged the distance to the other side. Maybe?

I wanted to go. Also, I'm not the smartest guy, a lot of people will attest to that. I waded in the water with the strong swimmers. They soon left me behind. I persevered, kept going. Somewhere before the middle the channel I started to weaken. The current was getting strong. Out there by myself. I knew I was alone. Fully conscious of my situation, made a decision. I have to go back.

Question. Do I have enough gas to make it? That's when I hear it. A cry. "I can't make it." Whinny voice. Heard it again, "I can't make it."

I turned. There was this guy Dick, floundering in the water a ways back. He had been following me. Bad choice.

"I can't make it. I can't make it." Looking at me. Dog paddling. I could see fear in his eyes. Whining, "I can't make it, can't make it."

Honestly. Me, for a young kid, I grasped the situation immediately. Looking at the far shore. This is what I thought.

I didn't have enough strength to get us both back. I could leave him to drown or stay and drown with him. I was only 17 years old. I swear, that is what I thought.

Panic!!! My mind was screaming at me from all directions. Fear in my brain and heart. I didn't leave him. Why?

I approached him from the rear so he could not grab me. I started pushing him, going under. Yelling at him to keep paddling. Keeping him afloat trying to move him toward shore. Pleading with him to keep going, keep paddling. I could feel it, he was getting weaker, not trying, giving up, making noises like a baby. He didn't panic, didn't try to grab me, he was just there.

Pushing him, there was no end to it.

I had no concept of time, no idea where we were, my head was under water all the time keeping him up trying to keep him afloat, yelling at him. I started to curse at him. Insult him. Called him everything from a weak little baby, a quitter, to a lousy coward and much more, repeating and repeating. Anything to spur him on, keep him going. Unaware the current was carrying us.

Can't describe the pain, how tired my arms and legs were. My mind struggling. Wanted to give him up. Couldn't. For some reason I couldn't leave him.

Both of us were going to die. I knew it. Must have been that fear that kept me going.

The current carried us into a cove were boats were anchored. We were a long long way from shore. I was pushing him keeping his head above water. How much longer.

I started to yell for help. Swallowing water, coughing, spitting, dead tired, keeping him going, keeping him up. A small boat came. Threw out a life preserver. I gave it to Dick. He flopped on it.

I remember the look on his face, in his eyes at that moment. Looking at me, safe on the preserver. I can't describe the look, a craven look showing only concern for himself. I don't think he would have shared the preserver with me.

I was so tired I had to rest. Fully conscious of what I was doing I let my arms rest and sank in the water.

I touched bottom! Just over head deep. The men in the boat had whimpering Dick on board. I told them I didn't need help. I pole vaulted my way to shallow water and walked to the beach.

A crowd of bathers on the shore, all smiling, looking at me, let me pass. I had been yelling for help. They heard me. Now, here I am, walking right by them. The little boy who cried wolf. My embarrassment masked my fatigue.

Made my way back to my friends. A long walk on a road.

Never said a word to anyone. Collapsed on the sand and slept.

Don't know how long I slept but Dick had returned. The Boat people brought him to shore. He was dressed in white duck pants, sandals with a blue "T" shirt. Telling the guys of the nice people he met who fed and entertained him. Never mentioning our ordeal in the water.

He was not one of the regular guys so my friends never questioned him. I never said a word, then, or for the rest of my life.

Now here's the mystery. This guy Dick never spoke to me or came around again.

I'd see him. He would drop his eyes, turn his head, cross the street to avoid me. That's the mystery. Why? I never said a word to anyone. Gone from my memory.

Why? Why did he avoid me?

Over 60 years passed. Sitting with my buddy Nick one evening sipping a beefeater. I remembered. I remembered the terror of that swimming incident. I told Nick. Nick was a tough talking New York City Italian who I loved like a brother. Nick and I were the last of the 6. Nick is gone now too.

Nick raised his glass to me and said, "You dumb Irish bastard."

Nick was a linguist. No regrets. Still shaking the water out of my ears.

Introduction

"GI Blanket OD"

I was once unceremoniously given a GI Blanket.
Usually a source of warmth and comfort.
This blanket provided neither. A great source of
concern.
I freed the blanket from its restraints to enjoy its
comforts for a short time. My only regret. I did
not take the blanket with me when we parted.

"GI Blanket OD"

(SOP – Stand. Opp. Procedure)
(TDY – Temporary Duty)
(OD – Olive Drab)

The summer of 1950, I was in the United States Air Force, assigned to Strategic Air Command, "SAC."

The Mission of Strategic Air Command **was to counter Russia's COLD WAR THREAT.**

Note; In 1950. There was no other force in the world capable of accomplishing SAC's assigned mission. No Nuclear Subs then.

I was stationed at Fairchild Air Force Base, AFB, Spokane Washington. Half way around the world from England.

In August 1950 it was decided to send three of our obsolete B29 Bombers to Lakenheath Air Base England for a three month tour, TDY. Our Bombers were obsolete because the United States had disarmed after WW11 and reduced Research and Development. The Russians did not. Because of this, in 1950, Russian military in many respects was superior to ours.

Strategic Air Command was at a disadvantage. It had to use the Obsolete WW11 equipment at hand.

That's all we had. Therefore SAC had to work triple time to keep Russia at bay. It was not an easy task.

The TDY had a mission to accomplish. That Mission was to demonstrate SAC's capabilities to Russia. Those capabilities were. SAC can hit you from any place in the world if we have to.

SAC prided its self on accomplishing its mission.

Because of my training and flight line experience. I was assigned to go with the TDY as NCOIC, Non Commissioned Officer in Charge, Aircraft Engine Specialist.

Support personal flew Military Air Transport from Spokane to Massachusetts. To the Azores then on to England.

We set up quickly in England and got our B 29's operational, in the air. We were very busy, missions were being flown and time passed quickly. It was our first payday in England. Most of us were outside the Orderly Room in a long alphabetical line waiting to be paid. We got paid once a month and it was always either just in time or a little late.

Payday was a happy occasion. There was lots of joking and kibitzing on the line. It got quiet. Everyone looking up.

One of our B29s flew over with both bomb bay doors open, loose, moving in the wind. We knew the plane was in trouble. The Crew Chief recognized his plane. He left the pay line in a hurry followed by his Assistant heading for a vehicle to take them to the flight line. Everyone yelling their support. Emergency vehicles could be heard. They were already on their way to the flight line.

There was no joy left in the Pay Line.

The TDY was a small group of Guys living in close quarters. We knew each other and the crew on that Plane.

There was no place for us on the flight line. We would only be in the way, so we stayed in the Pay Line.

Here's what happened. The way it was explained to me at the time. The Plane, I think it was 981, was on a mission over Europe flying at a high altitude pressurized to around 8,000 feet.

One of the crewmembers in the aft pressurized compartment decided to take a nap. He laid down on his back in the 40 foot tunnel that connects the front and rear pressurized compartments. This, by the way as I was told at the time was a common practice. A way to stretch out and catch a few Z's on a long boring flight. At least on that airplane.

Each pressurized compartment on the B29, front and rear, has a bulkhead door between the compartment and the un-pressurized bomb bay. These bulkhead doors are always closed in flight. When the plane fly's at high altitude the compartments are pressurized. There is a much higher pressure inside the plane than outside. Because of this there is a tremendous force on the bulkhead doors trying to push them out into the un-pressurized bomb bay.

Boomm!!!! The front bulkhead door blew out into the front bomb bay rupturing all four bomb bay doors. Like a giant vacuum cleaner everything in that plane that wasn't held down was "sucked out."

The guy in the Tunnel woke up in a whirlwind. He was in a long cannon barrel being blasted to the front of the Aircraft by the pressure in the aft compartment. Looking at it another way he was being SUCKED OUT!

I understand he was sucked all the way to the front of the Air Plane. He was on the way out into the opened bomb bay and over board when he managed to stop himself. Not before losing his fingernails clawing at everything to stop his slide. He was lucky, no one could have stopped him. The pilot recovered and brought the plane home, which was no small feat. The guy in the tunnel was shaken but recovered quickly. I don't think he was ever the same. No one else was hurt.

Now, the rest of the story.

It was November. We had successfully completed our mission in England, it was time to go home.

One of our Aircraft had an engine with high hours. This meant the engine had to be changed. I can't recall now but I think an engine had to be change at 450 hours of flight time, SOP.

To change the engine in England before going home would delay the Mission. Unacceptable! This was SAC! SAC always completes its mission on time.

It's important for the reader to know. This is not story book stuff. SAC was at WAR 24-7-365 for a long time, 1950 thru the 70's, many years. The public never knew. In the early days, SAC kept the free world free. The question was, Can that engine make it home? Do we bend the rules and fly that Aircraft home on an old Engine?

Decision time. Once again. This was SAC of 1950. SAC Will Complete its Mission. SAC needs no one. SAC stands alone.

Of course we knew the world, the USSR, was watching us as we struggled with obsolete aircraft to demonstrate we can still hit "You," if we have too.

It was decided the plane with the old engine WILL go home as is.

The word "WILL" when used in SAC in those days seemed to defy God. It was decided that the Aircraft will carry a spare engine in the bomb bay with all the essential equipment required to change an engine. It was decided that two Engine Specialists will go with the Aircraft.

If the plane is forced down on its return to the US, SAC mechanics will be there to fix it.

The Engine Specialists picked to go with the Aircraft was my buddy Lou and me.

It was time to go. There was a rumor that the plane was overweight. That's because of all the contraband loaded late at night on already heavily loaded bomb bay racks. Including the Front and Aft compartments. And then there was Lou and me with our tool boxes. Of course the plane carried a full fuel load.

Lou and I knew about the over loading and were concerned. But we were passengers, 5th and 6th wheels.

It was night, about 2300 hours. It was raining lightly, maybe some sleet. Lou and I got on the plane and squeezed into the aft pressurized compartment. On the floor. It was close. I had never flown in a B29 before. Didn't know what to expect and I didn't get any help from the Flight Crew.

That's when I found out my seat was a GI OD Blanket thrown on the floor with my back to the bulkhead door. The Bulkhead Door!

No Safety Belt.

The lighting inside compartment was a very dim blue light, just enough to see. No one on the normal Flight crew was looking in my direction. At least they gave Lou and me a blanket to sit on. I should have been advised to bring something soft. Lou fared no better.

We were at the threshold of the runway. The engines were running, going through the checks. I was told that # 3, the old engine had a Mag Drop. This indicated a possible ignition problem. It wasn't a "High Drop" so the Pilots and the Flight Engineer decided to, "Take it." This was not uncommon.

The throttles were pushed forward and down the runway we went.

I craned my neck to watch the blue runway lights pass the scanners bubble. We were in the air flying out over the North Atlantic. You have three minutes to live in the water if you survive a crash in the North Atlantic. It was to be a long flight. We were heading to Harmon AFB Newfoundland. I had been told Harmon AFB had a short runway. The Flight Crew slept most of the time except when they checked the Engines. This they did with high Powered Flashlights looking at the trailing edge of the wing and engine exhaust through the scanner bubbles. I sat there very uncomfortable, unable to sleep. There wasn't much room to move around due to all the contraband.

The Bulkhead Door was a concern at first but I was so sleepy, I soon forgot. Somewhere over the Atlantic I tried to get more comfortable. I tugged on my GI Blanket. It wouldn't give. I found that whoever tossed the blanket on the floor had closed the bulkhead door on it. The folded blanket was wedged between the door and the bulkhead, definitely weakening the door.

The Flight crew had made it very plain that Lou and I were not welcome in their space. I did not talk to them.

I made some basic tests. As far as I could determine there was no pressure leak at the door. I could not feel or hear a leak, my ear close to the seam. There were other noises. If that bulkhead door blew I had nowhere to go but out. I prayed a lot. Lou slept the whole way. I didn't tell him. When the wheels touched the ground in Newfoundland I can honestly say I remembered to say, "Thanks." What a relief. Of course I fixed the blanket for the rest of the trip home.

I still did not like sitting with my back to the bulkhead door without a safety belt. A safety belt wouldn't have helped much if the door blew. I knew that. A Belt would have made me to feel good waiting for it to happen.

I have flown in other Air Force aircraft without a belt. Never bothered me. Just something about being so close to that Bulkhead Door. I'm sure many others have flown in a B29 in the same place I did who will say it was a piece of cake. They hadn't seen the results of a "Blow Out" or had to share their "Blankie" with a door like I did.

There is a lot more to this story, I'm happy to report we made it home.

I understand what SAC was trying to do in those days. And SAC did it. SAC did it with a lot of young kids like me. We were a GOOD team.

We struggled to keep those old bombers in the air. And we did. Use to think no one knew how Good we were.

Wrong! The Russians knew. They stayed home.

I'm older now and I am still proud to have served in SAC under Gen.

Curtis LeMay.

The B29's Lou and I worked on in 1950 and 52 were great Aircraft and I'd fly in one again in a heartbeat.

Next time I insist on a cushion and a bungee cord.

Introduction

"Dead Zone"

Only the lady on the Bus is real. Her voice still resonates. The rest of the story surfaced during my recovery.

"Dead Zone"

The other day I took the Loop Bus to the VA Hospital. My bi yearly checkup. It's a small Bus, the seats face each other. The Bus was almost full. I'm sitting near the rear.

A lady, about 50 gets on lugging a big purse. She is on the heavy side, chubby. Squeezes in next to me, makes herself comfortable, a little pushy, taking both arm rests.

Out comes her Cell Phone, up to her ear, she starts talking.

Talking loud, about nothing. One way conversation, Continuous, LOUD! The Bus is moving. I'm covering my ears. She ignores me.

Sitting there squirming, Can't move, no seats. Panic, I'm ready to punch her out.

"BAROOM!"

"What the hell was that!!!!?" A little Guy sitting directly across from the women ripped off a terrific fart. Real loud. "BAROOM !!!!"

I'm looking at the Guy. He's just sitting there dead pan unblinking. Gazing straight ahead with a little shitty smile.

The Woman, stunned! speechless, wide eyed, staring, phone frozen to her ear.

The Guy is just looking at her with a little shitty, up yours grin.

Wow! I can't believe this Guy. I haven't heard a fart like that since my beer drinking chili days. It was no little, "Excuse me," cocktail fart.

"BAROOM!!!!" Reverberated off the walls. Everyone looking for the culprit. The Woman, speechless. Holding her phone. Staring at the guy. He's looking back. Little shitty smile.

The bus is moving. She pushes herself up, "Oomph." Clutching her Phone, her bag, waddles down the aisle to the front of the Bus. I see her talking nonstop to the Bus Driver pointing back to us. She gets off at the next stop.

Outside the Bus I see her, waiting for the next Bus. Eyes wide opened, incredulous look. Cell phone up to her ear. Arm waving in the air. Talking furiously a mile a minute, spit flying, people looking backing away.

The Guy with a shitty smile says to me. "I notice whenever I fart people close their mouths."

Grabbing my arm rest. "You almost blew me off my seat."

He's a Vet, warring a Vets Baseball Hat. I'm in my Vets Jacket. Told me his stomach got screwed up in Nam and he has no problem ripping them off. Told me about the time he was on a long line at Sam's Club. A lady a couple places in front started talking real loud on her Cell Phone. "I let one go. Wamp! A loud one." "Loud!!? Was it as loud as the jewel you just tore loose here?"

"Oh I can't control volume."

"The Lady was aghast. Dropped her phone on the floor. It broke. I picked up the pieces, handed them to her. She didn't want to take them."

Looked at me with a broad smile. "Guess she figured I didn't wash my hands.

She took the parts and moved to the back end of another line, lost her place. Several others moved too. Smiling, shorten the line."

I said, "I was going to tell the Lady to shut up, but you're delicate method of communication is superior to mine." Winked his eye, "Works every time. I'm a one man floating Dead Zone. Really helps fishing. Let one go in the middle of a lake. Better than chum."

He's a Vet on his way to the Hospital for treatment."

Hope they don't fix your farter." This time with a big smile, "It's the only thing I got out of Nam. Oh yeah, that and a Purple Heart."

We shook hands. Two Vets. There's just a few of us left. He is one of a kind. Glad he's on my side. God is laughing with us. God Bless the Vets. The Government won't. Wish I could fart like that. Maybe I could shut you up.

Introduction

"The Power of the Gong"

A Story about common street language.

Warning

This Story is intended for mature readers only.

If you violate this warning you are on your own.

"The Power of the Gong"

There were six of us. Teen agers, 16, 17 years old.

Growing up in NYC. Not that location matters, it's the same for kids, young Boys everywhere.

It was happening fast. We were changing. We weren't little kids anymore. Exposed to new things, new people, new surroundings. High School. Changing.

With this change came a change in language.

*Bad language crept into our vocabulary, conversations. We were becoming Big Boys.

Our Big Boy Bad language included all the choice four letter curse words. At first we heard these new words inter our conversations. Used more and more we didn't hear them anymore. We were Big Boy's now.

"Fuck" became the biggest punctuator in all our conversations. Got to the point where Fuck was being use to emphasize everything. This became common practice.

One evening, we were standing on our favorite street corner talking. Of course, in our conversation we were using the Fuck word freely.

Willy, the quite reserved smallest guy of the group suddenly raised his hands, almost shouted, "Wait a minute, Wait aaaaminute!" Got our attention. We all smiled, one of the Guys jokingly held up his arm, "Let Willy talk."

Willy, Glaring at everyone, "All I get out of our conversations now days is Fuck, Fuck, Fuck."

Silence! This revelation, coming from Willy? Stop us cold.

Of course we were aware of our new Big Boy Vocabulary but no one had ever challenged it.

Willy, Still Glaring. "That's all I hear. Fuck this, Fuck that." "You Guys can't talk any more without Fucking something." "Using Fuck all the time"

Coming out of Willy, the Fuck word didn't sound right. Willy, still Glaring, fist clinched.

"Tell me! what the Fuck does Fuck mean!?"

Daring, everyone. Looking one to the other.

Hands up, "We're stunting ourselves, we're never going to grow up past Fuck! We're putting a Tourniquet on our brains."

Silence. None of us said a word. Self-conscious.

It was evident Willy had been thinking about Fuck for a while.

Willy pointed it out. We all agreed. There was too much Fucking going on. Was it a problem? Our silence said, YES!

Willy had our attention. Softer tone, "We got to clean up our language." "Won't be easy. It's a group problem. Gotta clean it up it as a group." Still in the middle, Willy took charge. Positive tone.

"This is what we're gonna to do. From now on, looking at all of us, when one of us says the Fuck word, the rest of us are all going to say, Gong! Gong! Gong! To Punctuate it."

That got a rise out of all of us! A loud discussion.

Willy said forcefully, "It's the only way we can do it as a group."

We felt foolish at first, but we started Gonging. Soon a Gong included a tap on the head.

After a while the Gongs sounded inside us, simultaneously as the word was spoken. We started Gonging ourselves.

In a few weeks our Gonging grew quite. A few months Our Gongs were Mute. Fuck was gone.

The Gongs cleaned up our other language too.

I am 85 years old. The word Fuck is still in my vocabulary but scarcely used since I was 16/17.

"Fuck" has a place in our vocabulary just as long as it is kept on a leash. The Gong still goes off in my head when I hear the Fuck word loudly use in Someone's conversation, continuous depending on the orator.

"Fuck," never an enhancement. Indicator of a person's content, Never said in front of your Mother.

I don't object to the limitation of others. But I would recommend a Gong used as needed. Perhaps a National Movement?

Willy is gone but his Gong still sounds in my memory. I'm the last one. Writing this story maybe a Gong will find someone else, a reader, to annoy. "The Gong be with you."

Sweet dreams.

PS *Bad Language, Depending on your point of view.

Introduction

"Timmy and the Ghost"

Story of a young boy learning the values of life

"Timmy and the Ghost"

—⚏—

Chapter 1

Timmy is six years old. He lives with his Mom and Dad in the Big City.

Tim's Mom and Dad both work. Tim's Mom doesn't want to put Tim in a Care Center during Summer Vacation. So Timmy happily spends his summers with his grandparents on their farm.

That's ok with Tim, he really enjoys living in the country.

Timmy knows his Grandmother is his Mothers Mother. Tim is not sure what that means. He knows they love each other and that's why Grandma and Grandpa love him.

His Mother and Father talk to him every evening on the phone and his Mother visits every weekend. His Father can't make it all the time, never misses more than a week. One day Timmy's Grandfather, a hardened rancher farmer, reached out, took hold of Tim, turned him around by the shoulders. "How old are you Tim?" "Six years old Grandpa." Grandpa rubbed Tim's head, "I think it's about time to show you our magic place." Grandpa winked at Grandma, "Yup! I think it's time." Tim sat up bright eyed, "Magic

Place!?" "Yup." Excited, "Where Grandpa!!?, Where!!?" "I'm going to show you," taking Tim's arm.

Out to the barn, a beautiful summer afternoon. "We'll take the buggy. Old Bessie can use the exercise." Timmy watched his Grandfather hitch Bessie to the buggy. "Today Tim we're going to a special place." Lifting Timmy up onto the buggy. Grandpa got up, "Sit up here with me Tim." Tim happily scrambled up beside Grandpa. "Giddy up." A clicking sound in his cheek, Bessie started. Tim liked sitting close to Grandpa.

Grandpa drove the buggy along a fenced in field talking the whole time. Timmy holding onto his bumping seat loved it. Grandpa leaned over and asked Timmy if he had ever heard of an Oasis?

"Oasis? Timmy looking up. No." He had no idea. "Well that's where we are going, to an Oasis."

"What's an oasis Grandpa?" "An Oasis? Well, that's like a garden. Spreading his hands, a big garden in the middle of a big dessert. A place where there is lots of water, grass and trees." Smiling at Tim, "God put's Oasis's in the middle of desserts so people who are on a long journey have a place to stop and rest.

That's where we are going Tim. To an Oasis. Waving his hand. A magic place right here in the middle of all these big flat farmer's fields." "Gosh Grandpa, is it really magic?"

Putting his hand on Tim's shoulder. "This Oasis is more than magic, it is a special place that belongs to God."

"God? Timmy smiled. I know all about God Grandpa. Mommy told me." Looking up.

"God is very good and kind. Nobody has ever seen God, he's invisible. He's mysterious and he lives in a magical place called heaven." Grandpa smiled, "That's about right." "Grandpa? If this Oasis belongs to God is it heaven?" Deep chuckle, "Almost!"

Grandpa waving his hand slowly side-to-side all around. "All these flat farmers' fields as far as the eye can see are all the same." Timmy looked, the fields so big seem to go on forever. Some fields too big to see across. "Only one place," Grandpa pointing. Timmy followed Grandpa's finger. To his amazement, he saw an out ray of high hills abruptly rising up out of the flat fields.

"Gosh Grandpa, look at all those hills sticking up. Their so big." "Those hills are like an island Tim." Lifting his hand. "An island floating in the middle of these flat fields. There is nothing else like it." Timmy covered his eyes from the sun. He could see green hills.

"That's our Oasis Tim."

The Oasis became a green forest the nearer they got. Grandpa stopped the buggy by a fence. Looking at Timmy pointing to the tree lined hills. "We're here." Grandpa got down, opened a big gate in the fence. Came back to lead Bessie in, closed the gate came back for Tim. "We'll just leave Bessie loose. Plenty of grass and shade, she'll be ok, we won't be long." Grandpa took Timmy's hand; they walked along a worn path to the beginning of thick out growth.

Timmy looked everywhere. To his young mind, he was interring a dense green jungle hiding mysterious unseen adventures and dangers. Once inside its green canopy Tim could sense a warning, Do Not Inter, sounding in his heart. Grandpa reached down, lifted Timmy up, putting him on his shoulders, "Hold on Tim." Riding high on the safety of Grandpas shoulders added to his excitement.

He held on, excitement and wonder bubbling over. Grandpa started to walk up a hill on a path through the trees. Tim busy pushing the branches away from his face could see only green. They rested along the way on a big rock in a clearing. Tim looking everywhere. "Wow Grandpa, how far to the top?" "Let's find out." Putting Tim on his shoulders. Before they reached the top Grandpa said, "Close your eyes." Twisting his head to look, "Close them tight." Timmy clinched his eyes.

At the top, "Ok Tim, open your eyes." Timmy opened his eyes. There before him under a clear blue sky, a fantastic vision. Tim stared. His eyes quickly moved, different everywhere he looked. A multi colored valley, sweeping down to a big magnificent meadow. Covered on all sides by a continuous carpet of thick blue green grass. Wild flowers everywhere. Shaded by tall trees. In the center of the meadow, all most unreal, a beautiful crystal clear lake glistening in the sun. Timmy, A little boy, couldn't believe his eyes, speechless, instantly fell in love.

Sitting on Grandpa Shoulders Timmy looked everywhere focusing on the lake. He could see a beach on the lake side, a diving board, raft near the middle. A rope dangling from a big tree. More than he could believe, a little boys dream. Picnic areas, tables and fireplaces. "WOW." Timmy whispered.

Timmy was only six years old when he first saw the Swimming Lake. For the rest of the summer he pestered people to take him there.

"Timmy and the Ghost"

—⚎—

Chapter 2

Timmy is almost ten years old now. He doesn't pester people to take him to the Lake any more. He knows big people have to work. He still asks but he understands when they say no.

Grandpa says, "This is a farming community and people work even on weekends."

The teenagers still go to the lake but in the late afternoon after they finish their chores. They come home after dark, too late for Timmy.

Timmy stands in Grandma's front yard watching the teenagers leave. He calls out to them. Hoping one will come back for him. They never do. It hurts, but still he waits. It has been over three whole weeks since Timmy has been to the Swimming Lake. He really really wants to go.

He has been to the Lake many times with the teenagers. He knows the way. Grandma won't let him go by himself. He asked. She said no.

"No. It's too far. Too dangerous. If you get hurt there be no one to help."

After Grandma said no. Timmy was sulking. He heard an evil voice inside his young mind. Timmy had never heard this voice before. The voice urged, 'Makeup a story. Tell Grandma you're going to the South Fork. Then go to the Swimming Lake.'

Shaking his head to the evil voice, 'I'll be telling her a lie.' The voice. 'Not a lie. It would be like telling her a story, Make Believe'. Timmy has never lie to anyone in his whole life. He did start to think.

"Timmy and the Ghost"

—ɷ—

Chapter 3

Early morning. Rooster crowing. Timmy out of bed. He knew almost before he woke that today is his birthday.

Ten years old! Big boy. Excited, rushed down stairs to help Grandma.

"Morning Grandma, I got the eggs from the Hen House."

"Hey young man, don't I get a good morning kiss." "Oh sure Grandma."

"Grandpa! That rooster is still after me. He attacks me flapping his wings, squawking." Grandpa chuckling, "Tim, that Ol rooster just wants you to know he's the boss. Just swat him. Don't back down."

Tim made a face. "Eight eggs Grandma, two less than yesterday."

"We'll get some more by noon." Grandma reached out for Tim, hugged him. "Happy birthday Tim, I didn't forget looking into his eyes. Ten years old! big day. I'm going to bake a special cake for tonight."

"Now, sit yourself down. Eggs be ready as soon as you finish your oat meal. Say your prayers."

Grandpa reaching over taking Tim's hand. "Happy birthday Tim. You're growing up so fast, going to find you some big people chores." "Thanks Grandpa."

"Ma, I'm going into town today. See some Conservation people about expanding the Eula Dam."

"OH, by the way, don't look for any of the Teenagers today. They'll all be at the 4H-Club classes on birthing. Smiling, should keep them busy a couple two days." Pointing at Tim. "All the teenagers will be gone today so you'll have the whole place to yourself."

'Teenagers, all gone?' Tim was surprised how fast the Evil Voice came to him whispering,

'Everybody gone. Perfect time to sneak away. No one will know! Tell Grandma your story.'

Timmy quickly, almost blurted out, "Grandma I think I'll go to the South Fork by the Creek today. Do some fishing, look for arrow heads." Looking at Grandpa. "Maybe find Grandpa's pocket knife he lost out there."

Timmy had just lied to his Grandma. Looking down, uncomfortable.

"I don't like you going that far. What if something happens?"

"What could happen Grandma?"

"Oh let him go Ma. It's his birthday, he's a big boy." "Thanks Grandpa!"

"I won't be home for lunch Grandma, gone all day." Timmy hurried back upstairs to get his stuff, all the things he'll need for his trip. Tim looked at himself in the mirror.

He just lied to Grandma, a new feeling. He doesn't like the new feeling.

Grandma in the kitchen, he can hear her singing and humming an old spiritual song, one of her favorites. Stops at the door. Lying to Grandma heavy on his mind.

"Is that you Timmy?" "Hi Grandma." "Timmy, I packed you a lunch. I don't like you going all that way. Taking both his hands looking into his eyes. Please be careful." "I'm baking your favorite cookies; they'll be ready in a few minutes."

Grandma, so nice, he almost changed his mind.

"Timmy an the Ghost"

—∿—

Chapter 4

Grandma watched Timmy get ready, walked him to the front porch. He gave her a big smile, a quick kiss. "I love you Grandma." then he was gone. She watched him for a while, with love in her heart. He turned and waved, "He is such a sweet boy,"

For some reason she is worried. Timmy looked back at Grandma's house, saw her go inside, then he headed in the opposite direction for the white fence to start his trip.

A nagging guilt tugging at his conscience. He lied to Grandma. He deceived her and he knows that is wrong. "I won't think of it."

Timmy walked along guided by the fence. "Those teenagers are stuck in school all day, good for them, see if I care" kicking stone.

On his head a wide brim straw hat pushed back. A batch of his chestnut hair falls in his face. Occasionally Tim sticks his bottom lip out to blow the hair away, doesn't help. His short pants are old jeans Grandma cut the legs off and fitted them with blue suspenders. The suspenders fit comfortably over his shoulders. Blue short sleeve shirt open at the neck. Tim would like to go bare foot but Grandma insists he wear his Velcro sneakers.

Grandma's bag lunch stuck in his little back pack, fishing rod on his shoulder, he is on his way.

The Swimming Lake. It's a long, long walk from Grandma's house.

Walking along kicking stones, all by himself, seems like he has been walking a long time. Looking around, he is suddenly aware he is the only one out there. Out in a big big field. Out here all by himself. Timmy feels small and a little frightened. Getting tired. Maybe Grandma was right the Swimming Lake is too far. He has been walking a long time and knows his strides take him further and further away from the safety of Grandma's house and that makes him feel less secure. Tim tries to put Grandma out of his thoughts. He is getting near to the Swimming Pond, he can see the hills and the trees, he quickens his pace. Timmy's plan is to spend the day at the Swimming Lake and get back to Grandma's about 4 O'clock long before dinner. Grandma will never know where he went. He'll just tell her he didn't find any arrow heads. All the fences along the fields look the same. Timmy is sure he is following the right fence because of the path. The path goes all the way from Grandma's house to the Lake.

He sees the fence. He is excited. The same fence Grandpa took him to a long time ago. Some of the teenagers climb over the fence but Timmy squeezes between the rails. He grabs his back pack, racing along the path to the hill. He is tired but excited.

Timmy climbs the steep hill to the top and looks down at the Swimming Lake. He looks at his watch, it was about 10:30 AM. He is elated, "I'm here, I made it!!" Standing on the top of the hill, looking at the beautiful Oasis. Grandpa said, "God made this place for us." "Thanks God."

Timmy stared, "No one is here!" He started down the hill looking at the water. He knows he cannot go swimming. Grandma could tell just by looking at him if he went swimming. She mustn't know he disobeyed her.

"Well, I didn't really disobey her. She only said don't go swimming in the Swimming Lake. She never said don't go to the Swimming Lake." But Timmy knows what she really meant.

It is quiet without the other kids here. He misses all their laughter and shouting. The older kids told Timmy that the Swimming Lake is fed by an underground spring so the water is always cool and crystal clear. He went down to the water's edge and pick a good spot to set up his fishing pole but his mind is elsewhere. He was looking at the dense trees. The big kids won't let him go to deep into the trees. Tim stood up, "I'm going exploring." He went deep into the trees, climbing on to some big rocks. He saw a two deer, one was a baby and lots of squirrels. He did look for arrow heads.

Back at the Lake, it is so quite. No one is swimming, no one here. He spent some time skipping flat stones across the water and talking out loud to himself. There was a little echo he never noticed before. He went back to his fishing pole, there were no fish on the hook. Timmy had been fishing for quite a while with no luck. Grandpa said the Swimming Lake has been over fished and needed to be restocked. That meant there weren't many fish left to catch. Timmy didn't care because he still has trouble taking the fish off the hook. The day was very warm even in the shade of the trees. Tim tempted to take a dip in the cool water but he remembered Grandma.

He had the fishing rod wedged between some stones with the line in the water, he really wasn't paying attention.

Timmy ate his lunch. He forgot about fishing. The chocolate chip cookies tasted good, "Thanks Grandma." He stretched out on the grass. His young fertile mind was off to the wonderful land of make believe. He dreamed of being a Pirate. "Captain Fearless," The bravest Pirate of them all. Sailing his ship into battle, guns blazing. With a black patch over one eye. Sword in hand leading the fight. Then he was a cowboy, "Dangerous Dan," with his western hat pulled low above his eyes, his gun belt low, tied to his leg, ready to draw. He had the fastest gun in the west. No one would dare to pull a gun on Dangerous Dan. His horse, "Lucky" was smart and fast. Never lost a race. They would chase Outlaws and always catch them.

Tim fell asleep. He woke up! Something strange was happening. The weather was changing. The wind was picking up. He could feel it, hear it through the trees. His lunch bag blew away. It was a cool wind. Tim shivered in his thin shirt.

The sky was getting dim. By his new digital Spiderman watch it was three o'clock. He had stayed too long, he had to get home.

The wind was getting stronger. It was getting dark, happening very fast. Looking at the sky through the trees he could see dark clouds racing to cover the sun. In the distance he could hear thunder and see the horizon light up. Timmy felt a shiver of fright. He remembered his Grandfather saying the weather is very changeable and dangerous this time of the year. Tim does not like lightning and thunder storms. Even at home with his Mother and Father near to him he was still afraid. He is all alone.

Now he wanted the big kids to be here, someone to protect him.

Tim didn't panic. He knew he had to get back to Grandma's house.

He hurried to get his stuff. He did not take the time to wind up his fishing line, he picked up his back pack and little tin fishing box. He rushed out of the trees and down the hill side, to the fence and the pathway. He squeezed between the rails and ran along the path at the side of the fence, back to Grandma's house. He lost his back pack.

Telling himself. 'Follow the path and the fence all the way to Grandma's house.' It's a long long way.

Timmy has to hurry. He thought of Grandma, she told him, "don't go too far."

Tim knew She never wanted him to go to the Swimming Lake by himself.

"Too dangerous," she said.

The wind was stronger and colder, the sky darker. Timmy hurried, running alongside the fence. He looked behind him. On the horizon the sky was black. Lightning flashed through the black sky. The thunder shook the air all around him. It was coming from all directions. Getting darker. Timmy was running. The weather was catching up to him, wind blowing harder he could feel some rain drops. Big drops. He had to hurry. There was still such a long long way to go.

The fence line and pathway made several left and right turns. Timmy followed the pathway reaching out to touch the fence as he ran.

He came to Mr. Johnson's field. He could take a short cut across Mr. Johnson's field. Some of the big kids do it all the time. Grandpa told him never go into that field because Mr. Johnson keeps bulls in that field.

The bulls are wild and dangerous and will attack without warning. Timmy stopped and looked back at the storm behind him. The sky was getting darker, blacker, the thunder louder and louder. Lightning was flashing everywhere. Tim is scared, he has to get home. He could get there faster if he took the short cut. He made a decision.

Tim slipped between the rails in the fence and started across Mr. Johnson's field.

Timmy had made a big mistake. He no longer had the pathway and the fence to guide him, the only sure way he knew to Grandma's house.

He rushed on across Mr. Johnson's field away from the safety of the path and the fence looking for the short cut the big kids take.

He felt more rain drops, big ones. It started to rain steadily. The rain feels cold. Running and tripping on the uneven ground.

The wind much stronger pushing at his back, getting darker, the rain pouring. Rain made it hard to see. Tim looked back but the fence and the path were gone, lost in the rain and darkness. His heart was pounding, he is afraid. He knew he had made a mistake.

His mind called out to Grandma, "I'm all alone, I'm all alone Grandma." He could see Grandma standing by the kitchen sink. "Please, please Grandma, help me!"

The cold wind blowing stronger, whistling and howling, pushing him. His thin shirt no protection. He was wet all the way through very cold.

Afraid but still he hurried. Darker than the darkest night, black clouds covered the whole sky. No moon no stars. Covered by the black.

Confused, cold, arms wrapped around him. He stopped to look. Lightning flashed he could see nothing. He had tripped and fallen so many times he was mixed up. "Which way?" he cried out loud. "Which way to Grandma's house?" He thought it was this way but wasn't sure, he could see nothing. He was in a cold black place with nothing around him. Nothing he could see or reach out to and touch. Only when the lightning flashed could he see and then only for a second.

The storm getting worse. Timmy head down kept moving, moving to Grandma's house.

The lightning, always followed by a sudden cracking blast of thunder. Jolting him, almost pushing him into the ground.

Each time a flash came he saw only an open field, nothing, not even a bush. Tim, all alone, no one to help him. Crying, tears running down his wet cheeks. Still he trudged on. "I'm sorry Grandma, I shouldn't have gone to the Swimming Lake. I'm sorry, I'll always listen to you, please, I'm sorry," He kept repeating to himself. The soft earth turning to mud. Tim's sneakers were sticking in the mud, sucking at his sneakers making it harder and harder to lift his feet. He could hardly walk. He was so tired, all he wanted to do was lie

Down and rest. Each time he tripped and fell, it was harder to get up. Suddenly lightning struck right next to him with a thunder crack over his head. Timmy stumbled and fell...........

"Timmy and the Ghost"

—⚏—

Chapter 5

Timmy lay in the mud. Cold rain pouring down. To weary to get up. Cold hands, feet growing numb. Exhausted, too tired, just want to lie in the mud and rest.

He knew he shouldn't rest. Something inside told him to get up. Timmy pushed himself up onto his knees, too weary to stand. His thin shirt, pants stuck to him, his sneakers, gone, lost in the mud. Completely covered with mud. Very cold. Sobbing. No tears left.

Timmy's conscious mind is leaving him. He imagines he is home safe with his Mother. He feels warm. He is out of the cold and rain. He can see his Mother and hear her voice. She is holding him, talking to him with love, so calm so sure. She has him in her arms. He is safe, it's ok to lie down and rest.

In Timmy's mind his Mother is telling him about his Guardian Angel. How God gave each GIRL and BOY their own "Special Angel."

An Angel to protect them, to help them. His Mother is telling him his Guardian Angel will always help him. All he has to do is ask.

Timmy's consciousness, slipping back and forth. Tim, still on his knees, opens his eyes and whispers. "Guardian Angel, please help me."

He is afraid with a deep fear that he is going to die. Shivering in the cold, pouring rain the wind pushing him down. He cannot stand.

He was just a little boy. He shouldn't have gone to the Swimming Lake. "I'm sorry Grandma" He is so tired. Timmy looked up, cried out with all of his ten years of innocence, "Guardian Angel, please help me." Lightning flashed! Bright long lasting, jarring thunder.

An instant, a second. In the flashing light. Timmy saw a BARN!

A BARN!! Right in front of him. The door wide open!

It was dark again. Timmy's mind awake! Did he really see a Barn?? Is it real. Is he imagining?? His mind racing. It's black again. He can't see!! He stared into the dark to where the Barn had been. Waiting, waiting for the next lightning flash. The next lightning. Taking soooo long, soooo long. His eyes closing, his exhausted mind starting to fade, to slip away, eyes closing.

Lightening FLASHED!!!! Timmy stared. The Barn???

It's there!!!! It's THERE.!!! He saw it through the driving rain. Dark again. The image of the barn burned into his brain.

Still kneeling. Looking into the dark. His brain yelling at him, You have to get to that Barn!!!

Tim's legs, his arms, hurt, sore all over. Swallowing so much muddy water, choking, coughing, spitting, his chest hurts, sore from Sobbing. Timmy cannot stand up! In the dark. The lightning flashed again. He saw the Barn. It's still there! He has to get to it. Raising his head looking up to heaven through the driving rain. "Please Guardian Angel. Help me."

With a great effort he pushed himself up out of the sucking mud onto his feet and stumbled toward the Barn in the dark. Falling down, pushing himself up. His little body struggled in the vast darkness with lightning striking all around him, violent thunder. Silently he prayed, he kept asking his Guardian Angel to help him. The storm raging. Timmy fought the wind and rain. Falling down, getting up. He staggered in the dark toward the Barn. With each lightning strike he is a little closer.

Finally, he's there! The door wide open. He can see nothing. The Barn, pitch black inside, just as dark inside as outside. The only time he can see inside is when the lightning flashes. Stoop over standing just inside the doorway out of the rain. The swirling wind pushing him further in, he can't see.

Suddenly the rain turns to hail. Timmy can hear the hail pounding on the roof. He found the Barn just in time. He would have never survived outside in the hail. Timmy knew, his Guardian Angel saved him. The flashing light lit up the inside of the Barn through the door, the windows and cracks in the walls. Lasting only seconds each flash blinded as well as helped.

When the lightning flashed Timmy can only see half way inside, the other half of the Barn, far inside stayed dark. Shadows danced with each flash. The inside of the Barn seemed to be alive. Filled with moving figures that quickly disappeared into the dark.

The long walk through the field in the rain, the wind, the mud has drained him of all his strength. Very weak and very cold. Timmy is in a serious physical state. He is suffering from Hypothermia, Stress and severe Fatigue.

Just a little Boy all alone in the dark, in a scary Barn, shadows moving everywhere with the lightening. Too tired to think, his little body is finished, he can't go on. He must find a place to lie down to rest. Timmy looking into the Barn trying to see. Lightning flash! He could see Horse stalls on the left side of the Barn. He moved toward them in the dark. Reaching out to find a stall when lightning flashed. He saw a pile of straw in the corner of the first stall. He didn't have time to see anything else. He reached out and touched the wall of the stall. Even though his hands were numb. It felt wonderful just to touch something.

The thunder was booming with lightning flashing. Hail and rain on the roof. Shadows dancing everywhere. He heard noises from the back of the barn. Moving to the pile of hay, collapsing into it. All fear forgotten. Tim's reactive mind won't let him sleep keeping him dreamily awake. Timmy is out of the storm, inside the Barn. Is he safe? He heard noises.

In his dreamy mind he feels he is not alone. He wished he was home so he could hide under his bed. This was his last thought as sleep clouded his mind. Tim closed his weary eyes.

His eyes sprang open!! He heard a noise at the far end of the Barn. He is sure of it. Pitch black, can't see, he heard a loud scary noise. Soooo tired, he is sure he heard a noise, closing his eyes. BOOM!! Tim eyes wide open. Noises! From the back of the barn! Tim can hear them. All alone, frightened, coiled up tight in the hay.

Thinking, maybe one of Mr. Johnson's Bulls is here! Timmy could hear something moving banging into the walls. Lightning flashing, thunder booming. Too weary to be frightened, too tired to move, eyes sooo heavy. The raging storm in his ears. His mind racing in all directions, all mixed up with thoughts of his Mother, his Grandma, falling down, getting up. Will he ever find his way home? Living a scary frightening nightmare, half awake, half asleep, exhausted so tired. Timmy coiled up in the hay can hear something moving outside his stall. The storm suddenly intensified!!! Lightening flashing, ear splitting thunder, hail banging on the roof. The movement outside of the stall getting louder with the storm. The Storm in full fury. Lightning flashing, cracking thunder, hail banging on the roof. Suddenly! The Brightest Lightning Flash. Tim could see it through closed eyes. Followed by Ear Shattering Crack of Thunder. Another Blinding Flash! Brighter than the last. Ear splitting Crashing Thunder. From somewhere!! A Withering SCREAM. Timmy Awake!! Upright!!!! Eyes wide open!!!! Looking UP!!!! A Huge White Monster, a Demon, Rising up over him SCREAMING!!! Its Mouth opened wide. Teeth Flashing. Arms ready to pull him in. "Guardian Angel! Please, Please." The Monster, raising up, screaming above him. Timmy's brain stopped, closed his eyes fainted away.

"Timmy and the Ghost"

Chapter 6

When the Storm hit so quickly and Timmy did not come home. His Grandmother was overcome with fear. She feared that Timmy was and lost in the Storm, hurt somewhere.

Normally a calm rational woman she was imagining terrible things. When Timmy's Grandfather came home. He found his wife with her rain clothes and boots on. She was going out the door alone into the Storm to look for Timmy. That was the first Tim's Grandfather heard he was missing.

He calmed his wife as best he could and made some phone calls to his neighbors for help. Timmy's Grandfather, Mr. Johnson and four other men formed a search party.

They had been looking for hours in the raging Storm in their pickup trucks with big flashlights. When the trucks got mired in the mud the men would look on foot. They found no trace of Tim.

Getting their trucks out of the mud wasn't difficult, just took time. They were forced to quit when the hail started but had gone out again after the storm left.

Morning, the sun was coming up, they had been searching all night. They were tired. They continued their search without rest.

They had looked everywhere. They couldn't find Tim in the South Field. Now they were looking in the North Field. They all agree, little Tim could not have got that far in the storm, but decided to look anyway.

If they didn't find him they would get more people and search again. Timmy woke up suddenly. He quickly sat up, "OOH" he grimaced and laid back down. He ached all over. He was confused. His mind somewhere else. He had no idea where was he? He could hear people calling, "Timee e e e." They were far away but he could hear them. His mind wasn't clear, having trouble thinking. "Tim e e e e, Tim e e e e e." He pushed himself up, looked around. He felt strange, he didn't know where he was. He was covered with hay and he hurt all over. Slowly he remembered the storm. It came back to him in little bits. The terrible storm. The cold rain, the lightning, the cracking thunder, the mud sucking on his sneakers. Most of all he remembered how frightened he was. Slowly the night, the storm came back to him. A mishmash of thoughts. He remembered the Barn. Remembered seeing it in the dark, in the rain, in the lightening flash. He remembered his Guardian Angel. It was daylight, he could see! He could see! How wonderful, to be able to see. And it's warm! He isn't cold anymore! The terrible storm. He could still see and feel it. Being so tired. Most of all he remembered being scared. He remembered his Guardian Angle. "Tim e e e e e, Tim e e e e e," he could hear the voices calling. That's my name! They calling ME! There're getting closer but still sounded far away. He tried to stand but couldn't. His whole body ached, he was sore all over. He laid back down for a minute and then tried again.

This time he was able to stand, it was difficult but he made it. He leaned against the wall. His clothes were wet, muddy with straw clinging everywhere, his hair. So tired, face feels swollen. It not cold anymore, a little shiver, still shaking, a little bit. THEN HE REMEMBERED THE MONSTER!!!!! The Horrible Screaming White Monster! Tim remembered the wild eyes, the big open mouth, the teeth. He shivered. Where did it go????? He couldn't see over the high stalls. Timmy thought of the Monster. Was it real? Did he dream it? A nightmare?

Wide awake, NO! NO! the Monster is real. Where did it go??? I have to get away before the Monster comes back. Timmy standing, unsteady, leaning on the wall to trying to remember. He heard a noise! Something was outside the stall! Timmy's heart stopped. The Monster entered Timmy's stall and looked at him. Timmy eyes opened WIDE.

A Huge, Magnificent, Pure White Horse. A Stallion. Stood before him. Timmy looked at the horse, in disbelief..... My Monster. He looked into the horses eyes. They looked back with love. Tim was not afraid. After a moment Timmy reached out to him. The horse lowered his head to Tim's hand and then nuzzled him on his shoulder. Timmy weak could have fallen back if he hadn't been leaning on the wall. It was the biggest horse he had ever seen. All fear gone. Tim felt safe with the horse, secure, as if they had been friends forever. Tim knew he had nothing to fear. Looking into the horse's eyes Tim said in a weak whisper" You're beautiful."

"Tim e e e e e e, Tim e e e e e e," the voices called, much closer now. Brushing himself off, Timmy realized the horse had covered him. Pushed hay over him in the night to keep him warm. "Tim e e e e e,

Tim e e e e e e," the voices called. Closer, they were coming this way. Timmy, very weak, hurt all over made his way to the Barn door. Stepped outside. The sun was shining. He could feel the warmth. The men saw him come out of the Barn. They all cheered and ran toward him until they saw the big white horse step out of the Barn to stand behind Tim. Timmy looked very small standing in front of the huge powerful horse. Tim knew he was there. Mister Johnston quickly held his arms out.

"WHOA!!!" Looking at the men. "That horse is wild, unpredictable. He don't like people. He may trample the boy. Stay back! Gotta go slow." Tim saw his Grandfather and was filled with love. He wanted to run to him. Tim was too tired and something told him to stay with the white horse.

His Grandfather called to him, with the palms held out as if to push Timmy back. "Be careful Tim, there's a big horse behind you, don't move." Grandpa looked very nervous.

Mr. Johnson came forward and put his hand on Grandpa's shoulder. Mr. Johnson called to Timmy.

"Don't make any sudden moves Tim, that horse is a mean and he might hurt you if he spooks."

Mr. Johnson called to one of the other men, "Larry, you got your rifle ready?" "Sure do." "You know where to get him if he starts up." "Sure do." Mr. Johnson called out to Timmy again.

"Nothing to be afraid of Son, just move away from him very slowly. Be calm, we'll get him."

The big horse, with a low snort moved close to Tim.

Fearful, Mr. Johnston, "Are you ready Larry?" Larry had his finger on the trigger.

Timmy put his hand out and the big white horse lowered his head to Tim's hand. Timmy rubbed his cheek. Then Tim led the horse out through the men.

The men stepped aside. They walked a little way and stopped. The big horse nuzzled Timmy on the shoulder and then trotted away into a field. Timmy watched him go, the big horse turned once, looked back, then he was gone in a whirlwind gallop.

Tim turned, with tears in his eyes, on weakened legs, ran, arms outstretched to his Grandfather.

The tired men, astounded. A big mean horse acting like a pet in the hands of a little boy. They looked at Timmy in his Grandfather's arms. They had been looking for him all night. The worst storm in years. They were ready to give up a few times, especially when the storm came back. "How did he make it? Such a little guy. How did he come this far?" Timmy hugging his Grandfather as tight as he could. Talking rapidly without pause.

"Grandpa, it happened so fast. The Storm, the rain, the wind. I was so tired and frightened." Tim looked very small in his grandfather's arms. "It was so dark I couldn't see when all of a sudden the lighting flashed, and I saw a Barn." Timmy looked back at the barn.

Silently remembering how it looked when he first saw it.

"The lightning, the thunder and all the shadows." "It was so dark and I couldn't see. The lightning flashed and there was a big white Monster screaming teeth showing, raising up in front of me."

Timmy hugging his Grandfather, shaking, talking fast, repeating himself again and again. He was excited and the words just flowed out of him. About the Storm, the Barn, the Big White Horse. Timmy explained, "The horse was Whinnying and Raring up above me. He was afraid of the lightning and thunder just like me. He was whinnying. I though he was a Screaming Monster."

The men gathered around Tim listening shaking their heads. Grandpa happy to have Timmy back. He would be proud later.

Mr. Johnson came over to Timmy and rubbed his hard tough hand on Tim's head. With a grin he said, "Son. That's the wildest meanest horse I have ever known, and I've seen a lot of em. He's so mean no one can go near him let alone ride him and I've had the best Cowboys try. You are a lucky Boy. Twice! Once for pulling through that Storm and second for not getting kicked to death by that horse."

Mr. Johnson looked at Timmy's Grandfather and said. "You know I just moved that horse into this field yesterday afternoon. I left that Barn door open for the horse with some fresh hay. It was a lucky thing for Tim that door was opened." Looking up to the sky, "The good Lord was watching out for you Tim."

Timmy remembered his Guardian Angel. "Grandpa, I said a pray to my Guardian Angel." Grandpa hugged a little tighter. Grandpa looked at the men who had helped him search, his neighbors. Nodded his head. They all knew. A gesture of thanks.

Tim's Grandfather smiled at Mr. Johnson, "Guess Timmy tamed that big bad horse for you." Mr. Johnson grinned, looked at Tim. "Don't think Timmy tamed him. The horse just found a friend who needed help. They spent a hard night together. But you're right, I don't think the horse will ever be the same. Looking, I don't think Timmy will be either."

"The horse? I don't think anybody will ever break him, I like that! I'll just keep him the way he is. I bought him for stud, I'll just let him do his job and make lots of little horses."

Timmy looked into his Grandfather's face. "Can we go home now? I want to see Grandma." Grandpa holding on to Tim, "You bet." "Grandma is going to be mad, I'm all dirty. I lost my shoes, my new watch is ruined." Grandpa looked. He saw a weary dirty little boy with matted hair, ragged clothes, cut a bruised. "Don't worry about any of that. Let's see if Grandma will make us some hot chocolate. Then Grandma is going to clean you up so you look like a little boy again." Grandpa agreed with Mr. Johnson, Timmy will never be a little boy again, at least not the same little boy.

Mr. Johnson called out to Timmy, "Timmy you're always welcome to come over to see Big White. That's his name."

On the way home Tim said to Grandpa, "Mr. Johnson is a nice man isn't he?" Grandpa thinking, Mr. Johnson was willing to shoot his prize horse if the horse had made a move, any move. "Yes, he sure is."

Tim jumped out of Grandpa's pickup as soon as it stopped. He ran to the kitchen and met Grandma hurrying out.

Before Grandma could hug him Timmy said, "I love you Grandma."

Then he remembered how hungry he is.

Timmy would visit with the big white horse almost every day for the rest of the summer. The swimming Lake was still important but Big White came first.

Tim named the horse "Ghost," after he asked Mr. Johnson if he could. Ghost, little tamer now but he still won't let people get close, except Tim. Timmy walks in the field with Ghost all the time.

"Timmy and the Ghost"

Chapter 7

Several summers have come and gone since Tim and Ghost spent a stormy night together in a scary barn.

Tim, a little older now travels by train on his own to see Grandma and Grandpa at least one weekend a month.

Tim walks to the open fields near Mister Johnson's Ranch. Sits a fence post. Doesn't have to sit long. Ghost will appear. The two drawn together by a bond made through adversity. Happy to see each other. What they talk about no one knows. Tim started riding Ghost a while ago. Ghost said it was OK.

Tim can be seen riding Ghost across the fields, Tim low in the saddle racing to the horizon.

No one else has ever ridden Ghost.

Mister Johnson told Tim that Ghost will always be here for him. Grandma is happy Tim has Ghost. She gets to see him more often.

Tim sits with Ghost. In silent reflection will never forget how frightened and tired he was that stormy day and night. Deeply remembers how close he was to giving up when he called out, "Guardian Angel Please Help Me."

Miraculously the Barn appeared. Closing his eyes, he can see the Barn.

Remembers his painful struggle to survive.

"Thank you Guarding Angle."

He remembers the Lie he told Grandma. And the worry it cause her. He will never lie again.

He remembers Grandpa, all the neighbors and Mister Johnson risking their safety looking for him that terrible night. Can't thank them enough. He will never forget.

He also remembers it all happened on his birthday.

Timmy, Hugging Ghost's neck.

Looking up to heaven.

A silent prayer.

"You have given me Ghost."

"A birthday present I don't deserve."

"Thanks God."